MOVING STUDENTS
FROM POTENTIAL TO
PERFORMANCE

MOVING STUDENTS FROM POTENTIAL TO
PERFORMANCE

Dr. Dorothy Travis Moore

ReadersMagnet, LLC

DEDICATION

I wish to dedicate this book to every student who has ever crossed my path, whether in a small or large setting; whether we had a conversation or not; whether I glanced at you or not; perhaps we laughed or cried together, but your life has strengthened my life and I hope my life has strengthened yours!

ACKNOWLEDGMENTS

I am grateful to recognize those around me who have continuously encouraged and challenged me to write this book. I would like to thank Dr. Robert Pavlik from the Institute for Transformation of Learning at Marquette University for his wisdom and perspective. I am grateful to Necci Cooper for her editorial services and labor of love as I finished these writings. To the many staff members who have helped me along this journey, I say thank you. To my school parents, I humbly bow in admiration to you, for without you this journey would have been incomplete. To my family, my husband and my children who weathered the storm with me, know that I am truly blessed God chose you to be connected to me.

TABLE OF CONTENTS

INTRODUCTION

Many years ago, I started my career in education. I feel like I should start at the end because trouble rolled in like a flood. I want to tell you everything about the good, bad and ugly. But, that is impossible. Let me ask, who can fully understand life? You see a person dressed up wearing a beautiful suit looking smashing until you notice a button is missing. People usually will not say, "Oh you look gorgeous." They will say, "What happened to your button?" I am grateful for many things in my career, but a button was missing. What do I mean? There are no perfect people in an imperfect world. We do our best to step in the destiny given to us. It is not for judgement or focus on the missing button. It is gratitude for the privilege of serving and for me, it was children.

Every child has the potential to become something great. How they move into this greatness depends on the people in their lives. Teachers help move children to their destiny. Sometimes children live in difficult surroundings that do not foster learning and this causes a domino effect in school, it is not that they cannot learn. In some cases, no learning structure was formed before going to school. These students have potential, but struggle in academics and behavior, and they are considered at risk— we hear this term more often today.

Students who are not performing well are sometimes labeled as emotionally disturbed, learning disabled or juvenile delinquents. Most times they are homeless, low income, drug users, teenaged parents or victims of sex trafficking — live in single parent families, and suffer from the inability to read or solve math.

I plan to share the stories of children, young students who had to endure what many adults could not handle. They were born into circumstances, they never asked for or wanted. In some instances, their parents never recovered from childhood memories of despair and hardships. There is a lot of damage lingering in families, but there is no reason for the cycle to continue. I am an advocate for children who want to rise to their dreams. I never went into traditional education, it was not the perfect fit for me. I needed to give more to children who were labeled, forgotten, neglected, abused or worst. The ones with stolen childhoods forced to grow up too fast with no stability, no parental guidance and no resources. Most people are unfamiliar with educating at risk students or what it really means. This population of children are colorless (although a disproportionate number of African Americans are labeled as such); it crosses all races and nationalities. I have worked with many who perform significantly lower than their potential. Their outer surface may be touched, but inside they scream for help.

Note: Each chapter will contain some reflections I call TOMS (Tips on Moving Students). Moving students where? From the potential that is inside of them to a performance level that celebrates who they are. Just as TUMS can be used to treat the feeling of pressure or discomfort in the stomach, TOMS can be used to treat the feelings of pressure or discomfort in our educational system, as we work with our at-risk youth. Please embrace these TOMS because they are ideas, suggestions and thoughts that I have accepted along this journey.

PART ONE

CHAPTER ONE

WHAT I WALKED AWAY FROM,
I WALKED INTO

I never wanted to be a teacher or go into education. What amazes me now is that I have a long career in education. What is more amazing I remember the details of my high school graduation. Senior year was the happiest one in my life, I was finally leaving school. And I promised myself I would never step one foot in high school again.

School was stressful. The social pressures and events that happened during class was difficult for me— even as a good student. No more high school! I always knew I was going to college and as I was getting prepared— nursing was considered. I wanted a career helping others, yet undecided to which path to choose. Throughout high school, I volunteered for the Public Health Nurses and traveled with them. During this experience of working in clinics, I discovered its enjoyment. It was settled. I began to plan for a nursing career at the University of Wisconsin - Milwaukee. What happened? I did not like chemistry. While there I failed to attend the required laboratory classes. The result was my grades suffered, but I reasoned it was the university's fault. So, I decided to transfer searching for the perfect college and career. One thing for sure, teaching was not a bleep on my radar. This saga continued at the University of Wisconsin – La Crosse (UW-L) where I majored in social work. I noticed how majors in education had to complete student teaching assignments and activities. I thought boring and not for me! My pursuit in social work left me unsatisfied. Besides, the social work department was in its infancy and not fully developed, with that said, yes, I dropped out. Next, I began to pursue a degree in the Letters and Science Program. Speech and sociology were my majors with psychology as a minor and I managed to graduate college without giving any thought to my career.

In my last year at UW-L I received a phone call from the superintendent at St. Michael's Home for Children, he asked if I would work for his agency. I had no prior experience, nor had I applied for vacant position. I told him that I was flattered, and I did need a job. Then, I asked, "What would I do for you?" On the night prior to the call, UW-L had an international talent show that I participated in and presented a monologue about a family with a desperate mother trying to reach out to her troubled teenaged daughter. In an ironic twist, this former nursing student who changed her major twice had performed a skit related to education and it appeared to be the start of something with children.

Unbeknownst to me, the superintendent was in the audience. He told me, "I want you to do what I saw you do on stage last night." I accepted. The following week, I arrived to work in the young girls' unit. Unexperienced, I had to figure out what to do to capture their interest. I got acquainted with their lives to build trust using the approach of interaction. This method pleased the unit leader and she said, "Dorothy these are such therapeutic exercises. All of the girls enjoyed them." Simply by engaging the girls and taking interest in them—made a lasting impact. I stayed 18 months as unit counselor before the next phase of this journey.

A new opportunity arose for me to relocate to California and I decided to move. I felt good about my work with the girls at St.

Michael's. Something special happened there— my heart shifted to the point I began to reconsider that working with children might be a worthwhile career option. I reflected on my first year at the facility in Wisconsin—it was joyous and rewarding, but also emotionally draining. I asked myself, *Did I really want the same type of job?* The more I thought about it, I concluded that I preferred not to work in any kind of program with behavioral problems or emotionally disturbed adolescents again. The emotional rollercoaster caring for complicated and perplexed teens weighed too heavy. I decided to pass.

I moved to Sacramento and immediately started looking for work—any legal professional job with a decent paycheck. I found myself searching through the Yellow Pages looking for employment prospects. I was looking at listings for residential homes for children. The next day, I found a place called the Stanford Home for Girls, they had an opening for a counselor, so I contacted that organization. Again, this was not what I really wanted to do, but it was a full time paid position.

My service at the home made a huge impact on my life. To this day, I have vividly retained memories of sharing time with adolescent girls. One pivotal moment was an incident with a young girl who had a serious drug problem. It was around midday, when I received a frantic call from someone informing me that a resident had climbed on the four -story roof preparing to jump off the building— after she had flipped out on the hallucination drug, LSD. With heart racing, I quickly volunteered to go up and talk to the girl. It was an intense situation, not only for her, but for me too. Thankfully, I managed to calm her. Finally, after about an hour of reasoning, I persuaded her to come down. By time this episode ended, my body and clothes were soaked with perspiration, and I was exhausted.

One of the nuns approached me and said, "Dorothy, there is a need in our society and in our world for people like you, who can work with troubled students. Unto whom much is given, much is required." I never forgot the sister's words, though I wished many times I could have erased them from my mind— the reality was I could not. Maybe subconsciously, I did not really want to forget them! Her words planted a seed concerning the path my feet would later tread. While living in Sacramento I found a place to worship at St. John Missionary Baptist Church. One Sunday after service an assistant superintendent approached me and said, "You should go into education."

With an objecting look on my face I thought, *You are kidding me, why should I go into education?* All my life I ran away from education, however this lady did not know how I felt about teaching. Then she said, "Well, I have noticed that you are a good teacher. I have watched you in Sunday school class and watched how the young people respond to you. I think you would make a good teacher." I was not too interested in her conversation. One thought did appeal to me, teachers made more money than counselors in a residential treatment facility. The following Sunday I sought out that lady for a second discussion and found out she was a former teacher. Then, I confessed to her that I had avoided teaching classes in college because I thought it was not for me.

The lady looked and said, "You may have been running, but 'teaching' is calling your name!" There is a school in Del Paso Heights in the area of Sacramento with low incomes and high crime rates, I believe they can use your help." I had no idea what was next, so I hit pause and waited because the classroom constituted a fearful situation. The next month I kept thinking about this school in Del Paso Heights. Something inside pushed me to further investigate and I located Grant Union High School. I went to the district office to see if anything was available. It was a small district and I spoke directly with the superintendent. He asked me about my concern and commitment for youth and making a difference in their lives. We were on the same page as far as being genuinely concerned about students. Still, I had no training in education or a teaching license and informed him of my dilemma.

Confidently, he said, "Based on your experience, we can help you get your license. We have a classroom called 'Educationally Handicapped' with about 15-20 boys in that class—many are on probation and considered dangerous. I am going to be honest, many are behind in their academics and some are in gangs." He added, "I am talking about three to four years behind in reading and math. Would you consider working in that classroom?" I cannot recall my exact feelings, but something about teaching stirred up. Thoughts of a teaching career was changing from a negative to a positive. I told the superintendent, "Yes" and thus, my career in education began. The circle was starting to form.

TOMS
(TIPS ON MOVING STUDENTS)

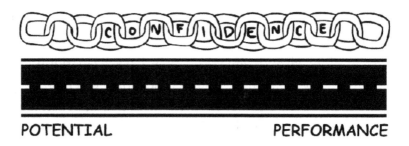

POTENTIAL   PERFORMANCE

- *Walk into your destiny step by step*
- *Ask the "Why" question*
- *Listen for your answers*

CHAPTER TWO

THE JOURNEY BEGINS

My first teaching position at Grant Union High was an internship. Brand new to teaching, I was thrown in feet first. Surprisingly, I never worked as a student teacher. Instead, I worked full-time while enrolled part time at the University of California to receive my teaching license. The experience of teaching boys was different from working with girls, I discovered boys were more mischievous. One day, I decided to place the boys in small groups to complete a math assignment when I overheard them plotting to steal a new Cadillac belonging to an older man who lived in the neighborhood. The ring leader, a student named Tino intimidated most of the staff, he thought that he ran the school. I overheard him tell his cohorts that he was leaving early but, I was not going to allow this. Then, Tino got out of his seat and headed toward the door. He was tall [6'3] and standing at 5'4, I was not a physical match for him. I rushed in front to stop him and stood there! With my heart beating fast I said, "Make one step and you have had it." Of course, I had no idea of what I would do, but I said it. We did a Texas stare down and Tino returned to his seat to finish his assignment. This was the beginning of many twists and turns of my educational journey.

After Grant Union High, the next teaching position took me across the Atlantic Ocean with the Department of Oversees School System to Aviano, Italy— where I worked as the Reading Improvement Specialist. In Italy, I pursued my master's degree in counseling and psychology from Ball State University's European Campus. After that assignment, I returned to the United States to Clovis, New Mexico.

My desire was to continue working with children and I became the head therapist at Children's Living Unit. It was a non- teaching position and change of pace working with children with special needs. I really loved it! New Orleans, Louisiana was the next stop and back to the classroom where I taught a seventh-grade class of slow learners at Woodson Junior High School. Each day I became more dedicated and committed to my students' welfare. There were rumblings among some of the seasoned teachers. They began to criticize me for working too hard. One veteran teacher told me to teach three days and take two days for yourself. Shocked and dismayed because that formula did not work for me, I signed on for five days a week. Even on Saturdays, I devoted extra time to visit the homes of my students.

Carefully, I observed students who had no concept or even wanted to follow rules, it was evident through their behavior. The tardy bell rang, and these students did not care. They walked the halls until they got tired. Enough of this rebellion, I decided—NOT IN MY CLASS! I arranged to meet with parents to solicit help with solving some of the problems—from that a reward system was instituted. I had 30 students and placed them equally divided into five rows with one student as the designated row captain. Every Friday, the row captain and their team planned the day's activities. The premise was the row that scored the highest would receive good behavior points with [one] stipulation, it had to be before the tardy bell rang and each student seated. The classroom dynamics changed, students were engaged and focused on doing their best. I watched student leadership and cooperation emerge, which from my perspective was a bonus. As I matured, my skills and confidence levels grew. I began feeling secure, competent and comfortable with teaching in classroom settings. However, my time was cut short— my mother's health was failing, and I had to return to Milwaukee to be near her.

Once situated at home, I began to explore career options there. In lieu of teaching, I accepted a position at African American Guidance and Counseling Center—although teaching had captured my heart.

Unfulfillment with counseling lead me to the Milwaukee Public School (MPS) Central Office. By then, the wealth of experience and credentials accumulated through the years positioned me to be hired on the spot. I was happy to be home and especially happy to be working at the newly constructed Vincent High School. My assignment there was to teach emotionally disturbed students, but the principal switched my assignment to teaching the learning disabled students. Five years passed with me as both teacher and Human Relations Liaison, then I searched for more options. In August, MPS announced an opening for a Student Service Specialist and I applied. Naively, I shared this information with about ten people from my school. I was told repeated by naysayers that I could not apply since I had not been in Wisconsin long enough, I did not have a chance, plus MPS already knew who they wanted for the position. Hurt and dejected I still wanted the challenge of a district office position, but my colleagues let me know in advance I would not be chosen, I redirected my thoughts back to the classroom. Yes, the rejection letter finally arrived.

Four months later, that same position reopened with an announcement sent throughout the district. This time wisdom was exercised, and I did not tell anyone that I applied again. I just told God and prayed, "Lord I believe that you have equipped me to do this job. It would allow me not to just serve one classroom, but hundreds of classrooms in my new role." I asked for God's favor and prepared myself for the interview. The next letter I received stated my application had been accepted with an interview scheduled. Thank God for my answered prayer. Seven candidates interviewed, and I was number one. Sometimes you cannot share everything with everybody. You must know in your heart what you want to do, then allow God to order your steps. The interview in December of 1985 turned into me reporting for work in January of 1986.

The first day at MPS Central Office, I met with Mr. Gerald Vance, Director of Student Services. Strong in personality he took the "get it right or not at all" approach. My job was to hold conferences with school administrators who experienced difficulties with their students. Sometimes, when students had serious breaches of discipline—the district held expulsion hearings.

It was not long before the district had established [new] weapons and criminal act policies. I did not mind being a hearing officer— but I was more concerned about what happened to students after they were expelled. To combat this growing problem, the district established 13 alternative programs to permanently remove students from regular school assignments. There were nine specialists and one manager named Mr. Phil Haddix. I felt lead to meet with him and express how pleased I was with the alternative programs that served our neediest population, but the programs should be named. Mr. Haddix was always a good listener and suggested calling it the *Behavior Reassignment Programs (BRP)*. With the director's approval, the matter was settled.

For the next five years, Mr. Vance appointed me to oversee the programs. My knowledge and understanding of administration grew under his leadership. He was a known perfectionist and if he gave someone a compliment, he was sincere. Honestly, I enjoyed the alternative programs, but I had a special interest in the Assessment Center and my goal was to learn more. I made it my business to find out about the referrals of incorrigible students and where they were placed. In the following years the Assessment Center pulled me by an incredible force.

When the administrator retired, I applied for that position and received the job. A whole new world opened, and I spent the next five years at the Lapham Park Assessment Center.

TOMS
(TIPS ON MOVING STUDENTS)

POTENTIAL   PERFORMANCE

- *Feel free to stand in the way of negative activities*
- *Don't be afraid to try strategies that are risky*
- *Develop classroom situations that involve student leadership*

CHAPTER THREE

WHERE THERE IS A WILL
THERE IS A WAY

I met Will in late August on my first day at Lapham Park's Assessment Center. School had not officially started, but I was eager to get familiar with my new surroundings before students arrived. I was in the building approximately two hours before an unknown student walked into the office appearing out of nowhere. I was sitting at the secretary's desk looking through files and sensed a presence near me.

Looking up and directly in front of me stood this tall, angry looking young man. He had on soiled clothes with unkempt hair and blood shot eyes like he had not slept for days. Without any formal introduction, he said, "They assigned me here," in a rude and arrogant voice. Unfazed by his actions I asked, "Who are you?"

Then, he snapped back in a nasty tone, "Who are you?" This student stood around 6' 2" with an equally large built. Not that I was intimidated, but concerned because we were the only two in the building and we were physically mismatched. With composure, I let him know I was the new administrator. His curiosity was sparked, next he asked, what did I do. Bear in mind, he still had not answered my first question, but I opted against being pushy, "I am responsible for the students assigned to this building." He paused. Then I slipped in, "Did you come to register?"

"No, I am not going to school a lot this year. I got to work, but I came up here because my probation officer is on my back." This sounded like a *personal problem*—I thought in my mind. Trying to get answers, I asked him did he come from another school. In a raised voice, he blurted out, "No" and told me he was expelled.

Great, my first day and a student with zero interest in attending school yelled at me. I let him know that I was not his enemy and wanted to help. Then, I invited him to return in ten days when school opened. Finally, he told me his name was Will and left. I ran to the files to look up his records and found a thick folder with his entire record in detail. Will's criminal record was extensive. It included gang involvement, weapons possession, five arrests, explosive behavior, two counts for battery, disorderly conduct, school expulsion for drug dealing, neighborhood shooting—plus two years of incarceration and he was considered dangerous. No kidding?

Well, I began to perspire a little and more thankful he was gone. I thought this was opportunity knocking on the door. Now, with the door opened, what should I do? I began this challenging work and challenging it was! The center's staff was comprised of 25 people which included a counselor, social worker and psychologist. Students were placed on the school's roster for one semester only. The goal was behavior improvement and to develop an academic focus to help them pass course work. Most had a history of failing their classes. I did not have a clear vision for the school, yet many directions came to mind. I needed to develop one that would suit this particular population. To carry out this mission, I waited for the staff to return from summer vacation.

The first day of school with the staff seemed very promising. They came with friendly attitudes—just laughing and talking. I thought, *This is a happy bunch!* Then I heard one of the staff members say, "I am smiling now, but I will not be when the students arrive." Not a good thing to hear because 165 students with serious behavior problems were assigned to the school. My responsibility was to develop a program meeting the needs of students who were drug dealers, gang members, extortionists, sex offenders, thieves, fighters and disrupters of every kind. It was important for staff to understand my philosophy, commitment and respect for their work. In our first staff meeting I shared the vision, and they were expected to teach every student who walked through the doors giving them the best educational program possible.

My opening words caught their attention. Everyone needed to understand, I believed all children could learn, including students who violated the district's weapons and criminal acts policies. I believed it was our responsibility to nurture, teach, train and bring out the creative gifts each child possessed. Also, I believed improvement in a school was a necessity, not an option! Every school must have vision. One that embraces the scope and nature of the population served. After speaking to staff, the reception of these ideas proved promising. The atmosphere was established— the stage was set! Together we wrote the school's vision statement and we were on the same page ready to begin the first year.

Will returned to school. He was tough and streetwise, also very accustomed to running things his way. He lacked structure, discipline and emotional support because his mother was not active in his life. In fact, she was a drug user and dealer with her own problems. Will started attending school when he felt like it. The street life drew him, which caused Will to hang out all night as pleased. He was unsupervised with no concept of rules. When he did manage to come to school, he had a hard time obeying the guidelines.

Will made it difficult and the staff knew for his survival— they had to provide structure in his life. They started small and worked up. Attendance was used to develop his accountability. This method eased Will into becoming more responsible. We constantly reminded him the importance of getting to school on time and the staff developed consequences for tardiness. This resulted in teachers successfully persuading him to buy into that learning was possible, as well as fun. I asked them to carefully look more at Will's specific behaviors and come up with intervention strategies designed to help him improve.

One of my techniques used was called *yoking the behavior*. This approach identified and prioritized negative behaviors—then tackled each behavior one at a time. It was not that other dysfunctional behaviors were ignored, but more attention was focused on the most troublesome ones. A rewards system was established to encourage the students to participate. After students managed to change a specific behavioral problem, they moved to the next behavior in need of adjustment.

Will would often use offensive curse words as part of his everyday language. Choosing better words was something he had to work on immediately. Other behaviors like walking in and out of class, whenever he felt like needed to change too. Will was a smart young man, but his non- conformist attitude interfered with his ability to follow rules. Will had to learn to obey authority. What did Will need? Structure, activities, participation with an opportunity to excel.

The staff came up with activities created for Will and other students to express themselves. They became actively involved and that raised their self-esteem reducing the possibility for negative behavior.

One teacher named Ms. Francis Gilmore decided to mentor Will. Mentoring proved to be a positive instrument for him. He became involved in the Human Relations Club. With his newly formed leadership skills, he eventually became president of the organization. He worked with the staff to understand how to become an effective student leader and enjoyed his new role. Respect was gained from the staff and peers alike. Will developed a new attitude. Instead of creating problems, he began to solve them.

By year's end, Will's outlook had improved tremendously, and his life was changed considerably. The anger left his facial expressions in exchange for more smiles. His favorite pastime was discussing community issues. He completed the semester with higher than average grades—moving in the right direction. Likewise, his attendance improved. and school had a new meaning for him. Energized by Will's success, I encouraged our school psychologist to get to know students and share some insights and information with staff to enable them to instruct their students better.

A Different Day, A Different Way

Every encounter was different at the center, each one had its own personality. I could never predict the outcome, but I appreciated the lessons learned. Our center was the drop box for children with the most difficult and insidious behavioral problems who were classified— as the worst population of students. One morning, I was coming down the stairs, I heard a parent denigrating a staff member and cursing up a firestorm. A student named Anthony and his mother showed up, she came to vent her displeasure with his reassignment there.

The front desk's assistant merely inquired if he could help her. The mother responded with an emphatic "No!" and told him, "You can't help yourself! Going from bad to worst—declaring she did not know why her son was sent to this *hellhole*. Like any concerned mother, she started to take up for him. She spouted off one complaint after another. With a disgusted look on her face she proclaimed, "This is a gangster school. Her unsubstantiated stance was he was not a criminal, no one could make her send him there and he was not coming.

Any layperson could conclude this mother vehemently did not want her son assigned to the center. While standing in the background, I wanted to properly assess the situation before I approached them. Thankfully, I managed to get her to lower her voice and invited both mother and son into my office. I wanted her to feel like her concerns mattered. Her displeasure stemmed from her belief that Lapham Park Assessment Center was akin to some criminal institution and it was not.

The dialogue started with Anthony telling her, "Don't sweat it mom," and she replied "What do you mean don't sweat it? They want to treat you like a criminal." Anthony tried to reassure his mother, he was going to be alright. His mother became angrier with each word spoken and wanted him transferred, which was not going to happen.

It was time to interject into their conversation with compassion and understanding. I broke the news to Anthony's mother and gently told her there were no transfer papers at the Assessment Center. Each student reasons for reassignment varied, so I asked, why was her son sent to the center. The real conversation began. She explained that he had a fight at the bus stop after being picked on for a long time. Stunned and disheartened by her next statement that she told him, the next time somebody messed with him to "blow their heads off." It took a few minutes to process and I replied, "That is a pretty strong statement, what happened?"

She went on to say [these] boys always bullied her son and he took her boyfriend's gun— then she unapologetically made it known, he had a right to. Anthony's mother revealed he spent time in jail, from that I got a feel of the situation. After hearing this, I asked was he expelled from school and she confirmed it. *Dear God*, I thought, *what am I dealing with here?*

Before she could speak another word, I stated the school district wants to ensure Anthony does not bring another gun to school. Initially, I had not looked at the records, but once I did, the files indicated he had shot another boy— something she neglected to disclose. I almost had to grasp for air when I read that. No one was killed; however, this situation could have been more dangerous for everyone involved and I let her know that he must be enrolled in this program.

Anthony had a chance to explain his side surrounding the incident and sounded remorseful for his actions. The daily harassment, bullying and name calling pushed him over the edge. Anthony inquired about the school's start time. I told him he could start the next morning at 8:00 AM. His mother never ceased her protest. Anthony's reaction to his mother's outburst was thought-provoking when he yelled, "Maybe if you stop drinking, maybe you could make some better decisions! Come on!" Then he and his speechless mother left.

I would never condone violence and education has no place for it, but the reality is gun violence found its way into schools long ago. Truthfully, I felt sorry for what Anthony had to endure. His mother failed to realize — the center was Anthony's last chance in the educational system. No matter what bad choices he made, she was the [main] catalyst behind his predicament. The irresponsible advice concerning street vengeance was not the correct answer to his problems. I believed wholeheartedly, she thought she was doing what was best to stop other kids from taunting her child. Anthony's assignment there was partially her fault and she lost the privilege to choose his school. Clearly, I saw a mother's love, and no one can fault her for that. Unfortunately, that situation mirrored many others with parents who shared the same sentiment. I believed that the parents realization of their child not being educated terrified them, and lost rights of school choice exacerbated these feelings. Most regular schools offered open enrollment for parents to select the school for their children. This was not the case with the Assessment Center, students were not given a choice—it was an administrative decision with very few changes, if any. Resistance was pretty much the norm at intake—with maybe the occasional exception.

This required me to work relentlessly to offer parents some degree of comfort about the school's program and I never once met a smiling face at an intake conference. If a student landed at the Lapham Park Assessment Center—the next step meant total expulsion from the educational system. It was hard for parents to admit their child was considered behaviorally dysfunctional and even harder to admit the role they might have played. These parents recognized the seriousness of their child's actions that caused their removal and they decided to challenge the decision anyway. I explained to parents how the behavioral adjustment programs worked guiding the student and parents into acceptance. The program had two main components; intervention and prevention. Intervention was designed to correct behaviors and prevention was designed to stop further negative behaviors. As overseer, I had to develop keen listening skills to better address each issue properly. I looked for favorable ways to ease the pain, helping scarred and damaged children rebuild their school lives.

Sometimes, it was necessary for me to be creative and use old theatrical skills to get a break through. Often this method was used to reach out and get their attention—then build a bridge of understanding and communication. I quickly taught students to recognize conflict and anger producing situations with avoidance measures that would promote positive and effective solutions.

If students remained disgruntled or irate, I would explain I was not the focus of their displaced anger and I wanted to help them. Calmly, I would tell students the only thing I knew about them was written on the paper in front of me, but I refused to treat them like they did not matter. These students had the opportunity to learn and experience success, if all parties involved cooperated.
Anthony needed trust, communication, relationships and a safe place to learn. Anthony had suffered a lot of pain, anguish —and rejection in his young life. We told him to trust the school to handle the bullies and he did. Anthony built positive relationships with students and staff. Our goal was to help him develop a new attitude about the consequences of guns and violence. Anthony left the Assessment Center with valuable lessons about the art of communication.

TOMS
(TIPS ON MOVING STUDENTS)

POTENTIAL   PERFORMANCE

- *Review records to gain insight, not punishment*
- *Believe in them and give students a fresh start*
- *Build understanding and trust, then drill school rules gently*

CHAPTER FOUR

A GENTLE PUSH

Another student who sticks out in my mind is Leonardo. Unlike Anthony he did not appear remorseful for his words or actions. Leonardo was smart mouthed and thought he should get the last word. He rebelled against authority, not because of any injustice that he received from us, it was just because. The first time I laid eyes on him, he was in a verbal exchange with his probation officer on registration day, to the point Leonardo corrected his every word. The probation officer told me Leonardo would be living with his legal guardian, his grandmother, but Leonardo would not let his angry rebuttal go. Students going back and forth with adults was common. This went on until the probation officer patiently told him— they would discuss this later, as he tried to turn the conversation to school matters.

Leonardo came from Ethan Allen Boys School after three years. He was an average student who refused to apply himself. He openly admitted his past heavy gang involvement and drug usage. Although he lacked respect for wholesome authority, he had tattooed a teardrop under his left eye representing respect for a slain gang leader. He was very articulate, but that was overshadowed with his boorish, harsh and offensive behavior. He was challenging, and we really wanted to give him a fresh start. Leonardo started causing trouble in every class from day one. The instructors repeatedly wrote referrals for his loud, disrespectful and disruptive behavior. Moreover, he was a negative influence on others in the classroom. There was no honeymoon period and his take charge attitude was overbearing. For the first three weeks of school, the staff was confounded trying to figure out how to turn this negative into a positive. At one point, they questioned if they had the energy to even deal with his temperament. Often, I had to work with staff members to encourage and reassure them—they had the strength to prevail.

Deep reflection of my educational journey brought back memories of the most difficult students assigned to the Assessment Center. Sometimes, hostile students made it easy for staff to forget it was still their responsibility to help change attitudes. Instead, they faced students who were ill-mannered and regularly hurled obscenities at them. Understandably, they became frustrated and discouraged—including the [good] committed staff. They had feelings too. Some had children who did not speak that way and here was someone else's child treating them like trash, and many times I knew they felt like throwing their hands up in defeat.

Nonetheless, my duty was to keep peace and remind them we chose this profession. The mission impossible assignment they signed on for may have been tougher than imagined. Their job was to keep trying until new inventive ways was found to help troubled students, even when there was not much to work with. They were always hoping to establish relationships that would allow connection and develop mutual respect with students.

Surprisingly, teachers discovered Leonardo had a nurturing side. He liked nursing. Who knew? This was contrary to his common displayed actions. We found out he had been caring for his little sister since the third grade. At last, we were on to something. We made an agreement with Leonardo that if his classroom behavior improved, the school would purchase books on nursing careers for him. Leonardo came into my office for a timeout and we focused our conversation on respect. I told him everyone wanted to put the past behind and help him become the best possible person. I asked him, "How can we help you become your best, Leonardo?" He did not know the answer. Then, I asked if he wanted to change? He said, yes but he could not. I refused to accept that, and Leonardo started turning his negative behavior into positive actions. After we talked, I asked our guidance counselor to spend some time with him to assure Leonardo that he was welcomed

The school created a leadership development program called *Positive Peers*. Students were the main participants with leading roles in planning our community luncheon [except] for choosing a speaker. They chose Leonardo to be Masters of Ceremonies, I will never forget that day. Everything was going well, when unexpectedly the speaker had not arrived. Unaware of this Leonardo went on to introduce the speaker. Thirty seconds passed, I was panicked in the back of the auditorium and thought, *Oh my goodness!* I had to quickly figure out how to get on stage before this turned into a disaster. Also, get the microphone from his hand before he became frustrated and unleash obscene words. I tried to maneuver my way to the front stage and Leonardo started to engage the audience. He was telling clean funny jokes about his family and the audience laughed. I could not believe my ears. I beamed with joy I was so proud of him. The speaker finally arrived, and our program continued. Afterwards I could not help but say to Leonardo, "You were so good. Why haven't you done this kind of thing before? You were so good and well poised on stage."

He looked me in the eyes and stated, "No one ever asked me to do anything thing like this." What a profound statement!

Before Leonardo came to the center, he had trouble in fifth grade and transferred to at least four different schools up until ninth grade. The ball had been dropped several times, which ultimately lead him to clashes with the law. Leonardo said "You're the first one that's given me an opportunity. I feel like I could establish a new beginning here."

I thought how unfortunate no one bothered to uncover the rich layers of untapped talent. He was labeled incorrigible early and others immediately looked for what was bad in him—instead of what was good. Leonardo was not incorrigible, he was misunderstood.

After that program, Leonardo worked hard, and his academic grades soared. He made the honor roll and stayed on it until he departed. Self-esteem, respect and focus was built. When he reached adult age, he decided not to remain in high school, instead he sought a program where he could get a General Equivalency Diploma (GED).

He completed his GED requirements and attended Milwaukee Area Technical College's Nursing Program. He left the gang life and contacted a community group who helped him get the tattoos removed. Based on initial contact, who could have predicted or even imagined that the loudest, rudest and most rebellious student would turn out to be caring, funny and smart. This was made possible because no one at the center gave up on Leonardo. More importantly he did not give up despite his circumstances. In laying adequate framework for success, it was crucial students in alternative programs feel welcomed in a new environment. The past should not be held over their heads and there should be a willingness to inspire, find new avenues and allow students to express themselves that create opportunities for a fresh start.

TOMS
(TIPS ON MOVING STUDENTS)

POTENTIAL   PERFORMANCE

- *Create opportunities when necessary to reach the minds of students*
- *Find a way to uncover talents and skills*
- *Keep staff replenished with encouragements and communication*

CHAPTER FIVE

MAMA DON'T ALLOW
NO GUNS AROUND HERE

Violence was on a steady incline with gang activity, assaults and weapons [guns] permeating through school walls. Lapham had its lion's share of students actively involved in gangs. Dan was no exception. Leading the center pushed me to become in tuned with school culture. I had to stay abreast of unforeseen problems that may occur; this day was not any different. I heard a loud ruckus coming from the guidance office. I hurried to see what happened and walked up on three staff members restraining an out of control high school student. This is how I came to know Dan.

He screamed at the staff to let him go, and he wanted to use the phone. Dan was told to settle down. He refused, reminding them a call had already made to his father who was coming there with a gun, then he insisted on calling his cousin to take care of us.

Dan broke away from one staff member, but he was prevented from leaving by another one guarding the door. Dan became angered and paced the floor talking about what his dad was going to do. Amid this fiasco, one staff member tried to explain to me what happened, while Dan continued to make threats of physical assault. Since Dan's arrival at the center, I never heard anything about his father. His mother brought him to the intake conference alone. Now hearing about this unknown man on his way to the building armed was frightening.

The staff tried to calm Dan, I rushed to call his mother to express my concerns. Well, she said Dan's father was known to do crazy things and advised me to call police. I needed to figure out what to do and asked her if Dan's father would talk to me. "It's worth a try," she said and gave me his father's telephone number.

I frantically dialed hoping to reach his father. Thank goodness, he was still at home. Talking fast I managed to get him to listen. His father never indicated that he had talked to his son earlier, and agreed to come to school unarmed.

After waiting for 30 minutes, Dan's father arrived. Let just say, he was not what I expected. He stood about 5'6, medium build and was not overly intimidating. Security checked him, and I greeted him at the door. He gave me the impression of an interested parent who had taken his son's distress seriously. I invited him in my office to talk privately. We discussed a plan to remedy the situation! One topic related to his absence in his son's life. Surprisingly, it turned out to be a good visit with his father.

Dan was so pleased that his father had come to school! He blushed like a little child throughout the entire conference. The father agreed to contact the school and help find ways to support his son get back on track. Explosive and hard core, but little by little, Dan let his guard down—at least in school.

The reason Dan came to us was because he lost his regular school assignment due to heavy gang activity. His records indicated at least three incidents occurred where gang members fired shots into student crowds—fortunately with no injuries. However, the shootings traced back to Dan. On the days he attended class, he openly mentored gang members in the cafeteria and refused to stop. The Milwaukee Police Department had identified him as the leader of his local gang. Dan was all about the "gang life" and he made it obvious—donning his gang colors all the time. Gang graffiti adorned his notebooks and tattoos covered his body.

At his last school Dan refused to reduce his gang involvement or obey school rules—this rebellious attitude inhibited his ability to function in a regular school environment. In his case many straws broke the camel's back.

We did not want him to feel unwelcomed or disconnected here at Lapham. The staff's sole focus was to change his negative behaviors without condemnation. Anytime the team met to discuss potentially dangerous students, Dan's name made top of the list. Like with many others, trust had to be built. We wanted him to understand, we were trying to help improve his position in life to become productive and not destructive.

In his weekly discussions, Dan often revealed feelings of being unloved with exception of his gang who most likely shared that same commonality creating the bond. Nonetheless, he deeply love his absent dad. Whenever contact was made with his father, Dan would make it known to other students who had to hear the clinging stories multiple times because he was broken and love starved.

Before Dan had completely abandoned gang activity, safety officers regularly spotted carloads of youths near the school. After dismissal, Dan would walk up to one of the cars, but would not get in with his crew. For the first time, he was concentrating on class work—not the gang! Things had changed, and students no longer feared him as much. What did Dan need? Love, family, friends, trust, a safe place and an opportunity.

We worked hard to build a safe, supportive and caring environment for even the most difficult gang members. Beyond building trust, showing unconditional love to the students and establishing a comfortable place was an integral part for youths with criminal backgrounds. Our slogan was, "We are not limiting your future because of your past!"

Dan was a natural born artist and loved to draw pictures for us! It was our way of bringing positive things to him. He was truly gifted. Like other major urban areas, Milwaukee was experiencing a huge problem with hand gun use. One weekend 17 teenagers were victims of senseless gun violence. Many local officials and ministers recognized this serious epidemic, and conversations took place all over Milwaukee with leaders and community activists. Everyone concerned asked, *What can we do about the guns and how can we help our teenagers?* The solutions were harder than the questions.

I brought those community concerns to school for our staff to gain insight on how to change students' lives entrusted to their care. The goal was to teach students that communities and schools were interconnected. Renowned Psychiatrist Dr. William Glasser believed children were only interested in things that were in their quality world. Survival, having food to eat and carrying hand guns to stay alive was in their world. Hence, the sad reality for many students.

We asked a lot of questions to find possible answers. Teachers required their students' participation to gain awareness and provide input. The adults were stunned by the student's comments and agreed that at the project's end their [students] remarks would be put on paper. Each student was encouraged to write a poem or short story about guns offering ways to make their community safe. The purpose for this school-wide assignment was to discuss ongoing problems of gun violence and find solutions.

We decided to write and publish our own book. Dan got involved and offered to draw the pictures, since by his own admission— lacked writing skills. Teachers thought it was a great idea for him to talk about his reality using another medium.

It only took Dan about three weeks to produce great illustrations to show the harmful effects of guns. He brought the subject up and asked what would the book be named. One students said, "Let's call it, Mama Don't Allow No Guns Around Here." Another student replied, "That's because you're the mama around here and you're always searching us to make sure we don't have any guns." Later evaluations showed that Dan's attitude changed, and he was driven by our mission and less involved in negative behavior.

The next few weeks, he dropped by the office with new sketches to see how I liked his latest piece. It did not take long before the writings were complete for our panel of judges to choose the best ones. Dan's illustrations were selected to appear on the cover and throughout the book.

I recall standing in the stairwell and saw Dan on his way home. I told him how proud I was of his illustrations, then noticed a picture of a young man who was killed for his coat lying down in the street and the shooter was standing over him with a smoking gun. "It seemed so real Dan," I said. Then, I noticed his new down-feathered coat. "Be careful." Those were my last words to him. He confidently strolled down the steps heading toward the bus stop then turned to say, "Oh don't worry about me."

Tragedy arrived at the doors of Lapham. The next day I received news Dan had been killed over his new coat, right before the printer called me to pick up the books. The news of Dan's death was devastating. Senselessly his life was cut short, he made a brave choice by trying to change for the better. I never imagined the picture Dan drew foretold his tragic passing. If only the person responsible for pulling the trigger realized, he had the choice to change too.

Students returned to school and I met with them to do grief counseling. Pain went along with the territory! Thoughts of sadness, dread and terror filled the school, students thought something similar could happen to anyone. We talked about it and I told them our book would serve as a constant reminder—the community needed to put the guns down. I urged them to respect people and their personal property without feeling deprived or entitled. If they saw something they wanted, they should earn it and not take anything that did not rightfully belong to them at any cost— definitely, not death.

When the book's debuted—the local news captured the moment and newspapers wrote articles about Lapham students writing it. Young talent should never be found in a grave, it should be developed, celebrated and shared with the world. The day Dan was laid to rest, our entire school attended his funeral. Most of all, the teachers were pleased they helped Dan use his artistic skills for good. We all had a precious keepsake to remind us of Dan in the form of "Mama Don't Allow No Guns Around Here.

Although it is impossible to share all the good works from the book, one poem worth citing came from Edward who did not mince words. He was sweet with words, but always in the middle of a commotion. When asked why his kind words were not used to talk through some of those problems. He responded that it wasted time when he wanted to knock them out. After a while, Edward began to trust the staff. Probably, this was the first school that he had attended where the people seemed real. Being authentic was important to the students. Educators must realize students can read their facial expressions, body language and voice tone. Here is Edward's short poem about guns.

I got a friend that has a pump shotgun.
Living in the "hood" you need one.
So, if you carry a gun, let it cease.
Because that friend I had, died in the streets.

Despite the aftermath of Dan's murder, the number of dangerous prohibited weapons students brought to school continued. Drastic measures were taken for added protection and random gun screenings were instituted. This procedure revealed more weapons found on Mondays and more disturbing, they were from our more focused and improved students. The ones who completed homework assignments, received good grades and participated in school activities, which raised the same old question. Why? To find the answer I asked an honor student named Terrance. I chose him after he was caught with a knife in his pocket— he explained that I did not understand the neighborhood where he lived. And he said, sometimes his mom sent him to the store late at night and told him to take a knife "just in case" and he forgot to take it out of his pocket. This was troubling.

I spoke to another student named Antoine his story mirrored the same scenario, he was caught with a .22 caliber gun in his jacket. He told me on the weekends that he and his siblings went over to his grandmother's house to eat because she had more food. His mother sent them late at night, and told Antoine to take the gun to protect his brothers and sisters.

Talking with students made me understand living in an unsafe neighborhood and the stress factor involved when trying to protect loved ones.

A decision had to be made concerning each student's fate. Having children who were determined to change and become better students should be given a chance. Students getting into trouble for accidentally bringing a weapon to school for circumstances beyond their control was not the solution. I discussed the situation with my security staff and worked out a practical plan that Monday's random screenings would be mandatory. Students needed to know the responsibility I had to uphold the law, protect staff and them. Also, I was not standing in judgment for their reasons for protecting themselves. To ensure compliance the school sent written notification warning parents about the new procedure.

The seriousness of students who believed they would be killed by age 17 or shot before they turned 14 did not go unrecognized. Further discussions led to students coming together to strategize on ways to improve their lives and neighborhoods. They made realistic plans for their futures by setting attainable goals, this opened our student's mind to make them accountable for actions or in some cases inactions.

I believed our students had a vested interest and should be included in some decisions. For us to be effective educators there must be student acceptance, otherwise the job becomes more difficult. After the book's publication, I could not keep enough copies on hand. Students wanted to share them with family, friends and gang members— everybody! More importantly, it was a tool used to start conversations with others. I felt it was a great beginning.

TOMS
(TIPS ON MOVING STUDENTS)

POTENTIAL   PERFORMANCE

- *Writing projects can speak volumes*
- *Help students make their voices heard*
- *Sharing with the community promotes healing*

CHAPTER SIX

EYES WIDE OPEN

Sometimes at the Assessment Center, I had what was called *Closed Observation Days*. Our security was reliable, however as an administrator—I had to take a careful look through microscopic lens for myself. On observation days, security would monitor our children's movements closer than usual to ascertain if students were engaged in anything suspicious or questionable. Security looked for mannerisms that showed unusual interactions between unfriendly alliances, congregating students and possible illegal money handling. Basically, anything that raised a red flag and looked outside of the norm.

Observation day was never without incident. We had a clash with a new student who had enrolled three days earlier. Originally from the East Coast, this young man Jarrod was energetic, and I was anxious for the staff to work with him. Oddly enough, he was seen in a corner with three other boys fidgeting with something in his hands—they found fascinating. When security cautiously approached [they] stiffened up and pretended to be talking about something else. Making sure the students were not holding anything harmful, their pockets were searched, and security discovered Jarrod had five bullets in his possession.

He was detained and escorted to my office. Protocol dictated that police be alerted to report anything of this nature found at the center. The police responded quickly and talked with the student. Jarrod claimed he only had bullets and did not have a gun, telling the authorities the bullets came from his brother. They gave him a stern warning and left.

I found out Jarrod stayed in a group home due to drug possession and a gun violation. I notified the group facility to explain the incident and was informed by a staff person that Jarrod should not be hanging around his brother due to a restraining order. Security continued to question him, and he confessed trying to call someone to retrieve a hidden gun in the basement. This lead to another call to the group home's director who immediately searched for the gun. Within five minutes, she called back to let me know the gun was found. Police were called again, and they returned to pick up my student. After, a two week detention, Jarrod came back to the center and completed his program.

Fool Me Once Shame on You

Police were called to my building frequently and it never became easier to see students in handcuffs being carted away. The deck was already stacked against them before they arrived. Sometimes on *Observation Day* some students would slip through the cracks. When you are responsible for at risk students, there is a high degree of danger, and extra measures must be taken. This caused my heart to sink inside, *Wow, I did not have a chance to service that child*. I felt like I had missed an opportunity.

The common denominator here was guns, guns, guns. Yes, another was one left in the boy's lavatory— this time it was a toy. Who did it belong to? I had my suspicions. I was not sure, but thought it might have belonged to a student named Donald. I never accused him, but he was acting suspicious, so I watched him. He would stop by my office unannounced purposely to make me aware that he was doing good. It turned out the toy gun belonged to another student. Later, I discovered he had prior knowledge and Donald did not escape punishment; there was more to the story.

This situation merited police attention, and I called them. The officers talked to the young man and in my words, *charged him up*. I had a good working relationship with police, especially the school squads. Since no real crime was committed, I convinced them to take the young man to his parents. Relieved and worried at the same time, a toy gun can be mistaken for a real one and get somebody killed. For example, a scared student keeps a toy gun for protection and has a run in with bullies—then pulls it out, someone with a real gun who did not know it was a toy might shoot. Another scenario, if the student gets stopped by police and panics then reaches for it to surrender, the student might get shot and killed because officers thought the [toy] gun was real. Too many things go wrong when real or fake guns are involved, also guns provide a false sense of security. Students want to feel safe in their environment and protecting them is an adult responsibility. Somehow, as a society, we have turned our responsibility over to them and it is not fair.

A social worker from the Social Development Commission (SDC) had dropped by to talk with me named Mr. Ron Johnson. After the incident with Donald I told Mr. Johnson about a student that I wanted him to meet. I thought perhaps SDC might have some social services Donald might be eligible for. I let him know that this young man came from a complicated background, yet had a lot of potential, but he was a trickster. However, for some reason, he became close to my heart.

I called Donald into my office and explained that his friend hid a toy gun in the bathroom that looked like a real Colt 45. Furthermore, I told him that prank lead the young man into police custody. I went on to admonish Donald about hanging around with students who break the law and bend school rules to remind him associating with the wrong people could land him in serious trouble, and stop any questionable activity immediately.

I had noticed a marked change in his attitude that I did not like. I gave him a firm list of dos and don'ts Donald let out a loud sigh of relief. Puzzled by this, I asked him what was that all about. He told me when he saw the police, he thought they were coming for him. Next, he started to apologize for bringing his play gun to school. In disbelief I said, "You did what?" in a raised voice. He tried unsuccessfully to justify his actions about being in another gang's territory and that was why he brought the gun. Donald was even smoother and more cunning than I had first imagined. We had already discovered one toy gun, where could the other one be? Although upset in a controlled tone I asked him, where did he hide the gun.

With head bowed and eyes looking up he said that it was hidden in my office inside the garbage can.

I looked and there it was! Mr. Johnson witnessed the entire scene. When I glanced in his direction, he turned beet red and ready to burst. I instructed Donald to leave the office. Mr. Johnson laughed so hard— but I was totally outdone.

Donald was in [big] trouble with me, I stationed him right outside my office for the remainder of that day. He could have been carted away by police too, but that incident I decided to take care of myself. No, Donald was never going to forget this serious infraction, at least not while he was at the center. However, once I examined the events of the day, my thoughts were, *Okay Lord, I see why I am here.* Since he took the risk of putting his toy gun in my office, there were indeed consequences. He was reminded these events would be different if I had called the police, and he owed me his life. Fortunately, Donald completed the program and went on to do some good things. Ironically, after he graduated, he worked full time as a security guard and attended Milwaukee Area Technical College.

Pick Winning Battles

Real guns, toy guns and knives. Another student Tim ended at the Assessment Center because he lost it in class and went berserk at his previous school. Something happened that transformed mild mannered Tim and brought about an abrupt change.

The report indicated that he walked into his classroom with a long butcher knife hidden in his coat pocket. No one suspected anything from this cooperative and docile student. Without provocation, during science class, Tim walked up to the teacher brandished the knife and threatened to kill him.

The students began shouting and the teacher tried to keep Tim calm while signaling for help. Tim immediately recognized the signal and warned the teacher not to move. Frightening for the entire class, security acted quickly handling the situation. Tim was taken into custody and later expelled from school. At the time, he was only 12 years old and it resulted with his juvenile incarceration for a year.

When Tim was assigned to the center, he was 13 years old. In a soft voice, he admitted to me that his mother's boyfriend abused him. He was deeply hurt from two places at home, and at school. His mother finally left her boyfriend, and Tim was happy about it. Also, at the other school the kids teased him, and he said that was why he kept a butcher knife. Tim had a severe case of psoriasis, it was not contagious, but caused skin eruptions in the form of flaky scales. The other students did not know that, nor cared and disassociated themselves from him. Tim's face, neck and hands were affected, sometimes it was difficult for other students to look at him. They tormented him and called him *alligator skin*, which we did not tolerate.

Assessments and progress were not one-way streets, I asked Tim what did he hope to accomplish at the center. Tim wanted to change and believe change was possible. My earlier conversation with Tim weighed heavily on my mind later that night. Looking for ways to unlock his potential, I worked closely with staff members over the next two semester to observe Tim to find his inner strengths.

I watched how recognition of little things helped him build positive self-esteem. It was not long before Tim became willing to work on his reading and math. He needed remedial instruction and was not embarrassed to receive it. He received certificates for his work and he was voted classroom monitor. Tim began to participate in group sessions that helped students focus on learning to accept themselves and others just as they were. Everyone working with the student, (including the student) must examine their reasons for being at the center and understand their contribution to the program.

To make a difference, educators must first believe they "can" make a difference. Teachers and staff must be encouraged to communicate with the families of students to recognize their likes and dislikes. Also, educators must learn to compliment students on the little things. What did Tim need? Affirmation and acceptance. Tim was ostracized by students for having a condition beyond his control, and he felt isolated. Once he was affirmed as a person and accepted for who he was —a closed world opened for him.

TOMS
(TIPS ON MOVING STUDENTS)

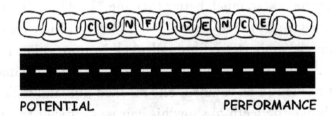

POTENTIAL   PERFORMANCE

- *Provide consequences for inappropriate behavior*
- *Make law enforcement work for you*
- *Find humor sometimes in serious matters, it can be a stress reducer*

CHAPTER SEVEN

THROUGH THE FIRE

I have talked about gun, knives, fights, threats and insubordination, you name it. The story of Ronnie takes on a different turn.

Ronnie was quite a challenge, he set a girl's hair on fire. Ronnie had been out of school for two weeks waiting for reassignment when I met him. His mother had brought him to my office for the intake conference to enroll him. Curious, I wanted to know what provoked him to set another student's hair on fire, so I asked Ronnie.

Nonchalantly he said, "This kid was in my sixth-grade class acted as if she was so much better than me." I told him that was no reason to set a girl's hair on fire. He told me did not mean to do it, but the girl embarrassed him all week in front other kids who laughed. According to him, she teased him about having nappy hair that needed to be combed. She mocked him and took out her comb— broke the teeth to show his hair was difficult to comb. He said, "I was mad, and I wanted to get even with her."

I looked at the mother, "Are you hearing this mom, are you teaching your son to get even with people?" She just shrugged her shoulders. This girl seated in front of Ronnie had beautiful long hair. He decided to take his brother's cigarette lighter to school and when the teacher's back was turned to the class, he pretended to flick the lighter closer to her hair. She turned around and asked him, "What are you doing?" He stopped flicking. Ronnie told his friend that he may burn a little hole in her hair. He warned her to watch her hair, it may go on fire. Ronnie kept flicking the lighter until her hair caught fire. Everybody started to scream hysterically, and he tried to put it out. The teacher came, and he grabbed a jacket from someone's desk to put out the fire. By the time, staff arrived with a fire extinguisher the fire was already out. Ronnie was escorted out and expelled. The story sounded premeditated to me. I shook my head, "How awful! Without the least bit of emotion or empathy, he said "I know." The school had every right to remove him. I was not sure about his enrollment there. He promised he would not it do it again.

Usually I try to have the child and parent come to grips with the seriousness of their behavior. Ronnie began to look remorseful. His mother stated his behavior had been discussed repeatedly. I informed him that he would be in our program for two semesters and must attend every class and counseling sessions for us to determine if he was fit to be enrolled in another school. Ronnie was placed in his classes, I viewed it as respite for him. He needed to get away from sources that angered him. He knew right from wrong, but at 11 years of age, he was still too young to process the full totality of his actions. Since, the Assessment Center classes were small he could discuss his likes and dislikes as well as family issues that bothered him. He was a very intelligent child and Ronnie soon discovered his value. His academics soared, and he led the middle school with highest grade point average. Ronnie became very likable because he received the acceptance he was searching for.

During counseling sessions, he journaled about the error of his actions. I began to realize perhaps he wanted to prove a point with the girl although it was the wrong way. He went beyond telling his teacher, mother or any adult about his bottled -up feelings, instead he deliberately used the dangers of fire to be heard. Meanwhile, he had to be constantly reminded of the severity done that could have ended up far worse. Drastic changes had to be made with how he approached students who angered him. Ronnie did a complete about-face and began to volunteer for activities in school and out in the community. It did not take long for him to be elected president of the student council.

Over the course of a year, Ronnie discussed proper behaviors that would defuse conflict and basic social skills. He wanted to formally apologize to the student he had injured and set a goal to follow through. Before he left the center, the day came when he did! Ronnie returned to a regular middle school, energetic and determined to do well in school.

Mistaken Identity

James had not been involved with the Juvenile Justice System, he was assigned to the Assessment Center simply because his school did not know what to do with him. He was constantly using the wrong restroom. When he used the girls' restrooms, the girls were upset and refused to use it and when he used the boys' they also objected and refused to use the restroom. For 13 years old, he was small, thin, effeminate and very insecure. Clearly, James was in the middle of a sexual identity crisis; he was like a fish out of water. Yet the problem with using the appropriate restroom had to be rectified.

When James entered the center he was confused, James' mother had recently died, and he was placed in the home of an older brother who served ten years in prison with no desire to correct his ways. James had two other brothers who were living under the same roof. His home situation required him to be tough—he was not, he had to find a way to survive. James rapidly began to deteriorate. Many days he came to class sleepy and lethargic; other days he cowered or brooded almost ready to breakdown.

I decided to call James in my office to ask him what is going on at home. He said, "I don't know. I don't smoke marijuana; I don't drink. But my brother and his girlfriend do. And they stay up all night long. Now my other two brothers treat me bad too. They're doing me just like the kids at school and tease me all the time."

Pretty much, it was the same scenario when James was assigned to the center. He would become violent, hitting, kicking and throwing anything in sight. The harassment got worst at home after his mother died. James revealed he felt like he was captured by the enemy with no way out. This child was held captive and not free to live in peace. His petite size caused him to be ridiculed daily. His mother was the only one who protected him from cruel taunts. Now she was gone. In his new living arrangement, James no longer had a bed. Every night he slept on the living room couch unless his brothers' friends came over. They picked on him and called him a girl and tried hooking him up with gay guys in the neighborhood for their amusement. "I'm not like that," he said. James was not gay.

James was a volcanic eruption waiting to happen, something had to be done to help him through his ordeal. He lacked the parental supervision needed to function properly. He was a child with zero guidance from any significant adult in his life. Once I discovered his grandmother was his legal guardian, I asked his permission to call her. His grandmother was 87 years old and given her advanced age did not get around well. She lived in subsidized housing for the elderly where children were not allowed. Quite the conundrum, I wondered how the courts would grant guardianship to someone that age, who could not provide a decent place to live or proper guidance and expect James to succeed.

We did our best here to help James flourish despite his circumstances. We allowed him to come early and stay late. The staff found out James was an auditory learner and loved to sing. They decided to focus on exposing him to positive activities in the community. One of the teachers volunteered to take him to her church where he could get involved in the youth group. This extra- curricular activity was contingent upon James coming to school on time. Before long James spent time at the neighborhood church and received positive reinforcement, which translated into loving support from church members. The pastor agreed to help with foster placement and this method helped James tremendously. The staff devised an individualized learning program to address his preferred learning style. Through his group sessions, James began to turn around. He started to develop some coping skills and the counselor became confident— he would be fine. He won the hearts of our teachers with his gentle ways and willingness to help. James earned membership in the Boys and Girls Club and became active in the local Young Men's Christian Association (YMCA). Before James was reassigned, the staff stressed to him the importance of filling his life with positive experiences and maintaining close ties with the community to keep him focused and engaged.

TOMS
(TIPS ON MOVING STUDENTS)

POTENTIAL   PERFORMANCE

- *Show acceptance but hold students accountable*
- *Look for potential and challenge low standards*
- *Seek community involved for resources*

CHAPTER EIGHT

REALITY CHECKMATE FOR TWO

What on earth was a 17 year old student doing in the ninth grade? Martin did not seem to know nor particularly concerned. He was labeled a chronic disrupter— aside from causing disturbances— Martin was a loner. I found that strange because most trouble makers desire popularity and usually are attention seekers. According to the file, it was crystal clear his mother did not care and his father was absent from his life. No push at all from the mother to get Martin educated — rather she wanted him to work to help pay bills. I had seen it all before when mothers would turn sons into the *substitute* man of the house, but never exposed them to positive male role models to learn anything. I would never suggest that she did not need the help, she was a single parent doing her best. Martin had no interest in education, but bragged that he was going to work a job paying $7,000 a week, not for a measly $7.00 an hour.

"Let me get this straight, you are 17 years old in school with zero credits and no work experience, yet you want to make $7,000 per week?" It sounds like you believe this world owes you something," I boldly said. Martin did not comment. Going through his folder, I read that previous staff felt Martin was a kleptomaniac. There were numerous recorded incidents of theft when he was around. All signs pointed to Martin—without his confession or hard evidence, no one could prove that he was the culprit. One incident occurred when money was taken from students' lockers and again Martin vehemently denied any involvement with the break-ins. However, he proclaimed that he knew friends who stole—not him. More incidents surfaced with Martin being the common denominator. During the conference, his mother revealed several neighbors complained that Martin stole money from children on their block. At that point, I told him to stop fooling himself; his feet were closer to the fire, than he thought. Nothing I said fazed Martin as he blankly stared into space, which I interpreted as unconfessed guilt.

Here again, I was not exactly sure how I was going to help him come to grips and rid his criminal behavior. I had my work cut out for me. Surprisingly, this unconcerned mother told Martin as they were leaving, "Martin, I want you to allow these people to help you."

The week after Martin was placed in a homeroom— I instructed the guidance counselor to place him in a group that dealt with the consequences of stealing and negative behaviors. A few days later, the guidance counselor said to me that Martin thinks that he is too slick to get caught. She thought of him as lazy and like most teenagers his age, he wants money without any labor or effort on his part.

I sponsored a Saturday school workshop with Martin and his mother in attendance. The local police gave a presentation about stealing and the increased number of thefts in the community. We discussed ways to keep our students on target. It was a great day. A catered lunch was provided to everyone who gave up their Saturday to attend. As show of appreciation I went to my office and prepared certificates for the parents. While I was printing certificates, a teacher retrieved me to observe parents interacting with police officers which was considered a "Kodak moment." Earlier that day, I went to the bank to withdraw $800 from my personal account to pay for services. I had eight $100 bills in my wallet. I glanced at my purse that was inside my desk before I left and figured everything would be okay for a few minutes. I stood in the conference room for about ten minutes and whispered a prayer, "Thank You, God for what You are doing in this place, parents are asking questions and seeking answers to family problems."

Thoughts of my unattended purse prompted me to return to my office. When I entered the adjacent area, the caterer Rose Hardy sat outside the door and Martin sat inside. The moment I walked in I knew my purse had been disturbed. My heart began to thump. I reached for my wallet— the money was missing. *Oh my God*, I thought. I asked Rose did she come inside my office and take anything. She replied no. Then, I had to explain the money I planned to pay her with disappeared. I did not know what to think. When Rose left out, one of my newer teachers entered. My distressed look caused him to ask, "What's wrong?" I told him about the missing money. He closed the door and said, "Martin has it, I know this kid he came from my old high school. He was in a work program at a factory on the south side. Martin brazenly went into the president's office stole money and a watch. Nobody could prove it, but Martin lost his job placement after the theft. That's the real reason the school expelled him." He was adamant about Martin.

I thanked him for shedding [new] light. I had been down this path before in dealing with theft. The police always said, *if you did not see it, or if you can't prove it, it could be almost anybody.* What was I going to do?
I called Martin into the office and directly asked "Did you go into my purse?" Of course, he said, "No." He was more nonchalant than usual, I would say *cooler* than a cucumber. I wanted a straight answer and asked him again— he insisted no.

Normally, security would search students, but this workshop was on Saturday with no one on duty. This decision was left to me,

I ordered him to empty his pockets. A total of $1.30 was in his front right pocket. In his left front pocket, there were about five cards, but no money. I was desperate. Then, I told him to remove his shoes. Nothing. Martin went back to the workshop where his mother was waiting for him. Finally, it ended with great success despite the $800 theft.

Wanting God's Presence

Sunday morning arrived, and I went to church to be in God's presence. I always brought my tithes. Now I am sitting in church having this quiet conversation with the Lord. I said, "Lord, I cannot pay my tithe this Sunday. Eight hundred dollars for bills and other things is missing. I just cannot do it." Not paying tithes worried me. I heard a small voice ask, "Do you trust Me or not?" Before the offering was taken, I whipped out my checkbook and paid them. "I do not know what will go lacking Lord, but I must pay my tithes, it belongs to you!"

Still troubled about my missing money, I stood up tall to praise God from the depth of my soul. The minute I opened God's word to follow the message, a clear vision went across my mind. My heavenly Father revealed the image of Martin showing me the cards from his front left pocket. I recalled a red and white card—identical to the one issued from the Educator's Credit Union. Martin and his mother were barely employed, therefore would have no reason to own one. I rummaged through my purse again—the card was missing. "Thank you, Lord. Just show me what to do next."

After service, I went to my office to the check files for Martin's phone number. I called his mother to explain why I was calling. With an authoritative voice, I told her Martin took my money and I was calling the police to arrest him and if he returns the money, he may get a lighter sentence. The mother gave him the phone. "Martin, you have my credit card, so you do not bother denying it because I saw it in your possession yesterday. Yes, I know you took the money. I am sending the police right now!" I declared. They are going send you to jail for 10 years," even though I did not exactly know what the law stated. Martin claimed not to have it, but I did not relent, "Where is it?" I shouted! Finally, the truth! He told me that he hid it. He confessed the money was underneath a cushion in the outer office near the secretary's desk. Mystery solved. I walked to the area, flipped up the cushion to recover my money. I called the police, Martin was arrested and sentenced to 90 days in jail. After his release, he returned to the Assessment Center and he was on probation for two years. I forgave him, and a different young man emerged. His academics improved, and he participated in the school-to-work program for job training. The reality [shock] of going to jail made Martin realized there was more to lose than gain.

Wrong Place, Wrong Crowd

One week rolled around and it was Sunday again, this time my heart was completely devastated by this next student. This December morning felt different to me. I had considered turning on the television, but I had to stay focused to teach Sunday school. Yet this spiritual push persisted, and I turned it on. A news bulletin interrupted the regular program. There had been a mass murder in central city Milwaukee. Five people were killed execution style including a 13- year-old girl, I stopped dead in my tracks to listen more. The news reported it was a drug deal gone bad. This event caught my eye because the young people who were involved in this drug incident matched students who attended the center. Thoughts of a 13- year- old girl who needlessly lost her life disturbed my heart. The next words from the newscaster literally crushed my soul. One of the young people involved in the slayings was named Elliot. "Elliot," I said! "Oh God—not my Elliot!"

I remembered this young boy who wanted to make something out of his life. "I want to be somebody," Elliot said. Those words pierced my core and I understood why I was moved to turn on the television. Once I made it to church to teach Sunday school, I told the class about Elliot. I asked my class to pray for the slain families, his family and him because nothing hurts more than seeing a child with potential go in the wrong direction. Everyone needs God's mercy. Pushing back the tears watering my eyes, I thought about our many sessions—only a few months before this gruesome incident. At 16 years old, Elliot had already served four years incarcerated, more than any other student at the center.

His family moved to Milwaukee from Chicago. Elliot had spent so much time behind bars until he seemed afraid of the outside world. He freely talked about prison and mentioned that time was not his own because he had to follow the strict rules. He was just a voiceless and faceless number, but once outside that changed. Now confronted with managing his own time in a new city was overwhelming. Hoping for a new start his mother relocated the family to leave their past bad experiences. I personally tried to counsel Elliot to make good choices. We connected, and he understood that school afforded him the opportunity to refocus, set positive goals and change his life—if he was willing to put forth an effort. Elliot began coming to school regularly. He would come by the office to keep me abreast of his classwork. Considering the years in jail—he expressed how he really enjoyed being home with his family.

Elliot loved to talk about Chicago. Every time I looked around he was telling me stories about his home town. He gabbed on about how much bigger and better his city was than Milwaukee. At the end of the grading cycle, the school planned a field trip to Chicago. I told Elliot if his grades were satisfactory, I would permit him to travel with us and serve as the tour guide. He was ecstatic and promised to make the honor roll. Given the odds stacked against him, I thought that might be a stretch for first report card marking, but waited for his grades. Like he pledged, Elliot's name appeared on the honor roll with a 3.0 and I kept my promise too.

On our bus ride through the Windy City, Elliot our tourist concierge happily explained everything about Chicago. I could tell he had extensive exposure to the tourist attractions—he sprouted off a lot of good information about the Sears Tower, the Planetarium, the Museum of Science and Industry and others along the city's sprawling 20 miles of lakefront. A few days later, Elliot stopped coming to school. His truancy caused the attendance officer to investigate and she discovered the family had moved back to Chicago. Saddened to learn this because Elliot was making excellent progress, and I had envisioned his future brimming with real possibilities. I never heard anything more about Elliot until that alarming broadcast.

During the next three months of court proceedings I followed Elliot's case attentively. I contemplated going to see him, but I asked myself this question, *What would I say or what would I do?*, especially knowing that five people had been killed and this young man was involved. After months of tracking the trial, that fateful day arrived for the verdict. Guilty. My hard-working, bright eyed, intelligent Elliot was found culpable on five counts of murder—sentenced to life in prison without the possibility of parole. I shook my head and cried out, "What a waste!" Everyone lost, the victims, the families and Elliot.

This child stayed on my mind. Two months later, I had to reach out to him. I wrote a letter and sent it to Waupun State Penitentiary of Wisconsin where he was serving his sentence. Waupun was a maximum-security facility reserved for hardened criminals, in a terrible irony he still ended up in Wisconsin.

The letter read:

Dear Elliot,

This is your principal from the Assessment Center.

How are you? I hope you are doing as well as can be expected."

When the letter arrived on Tuesday, he immediately responded on the same afternoon. The next day I received a 10 page letter from Elliot. The first page read as follows:

Dear Principal,

I'm so glad you wrote me. I'm so confused I don't know what to do. Please continue to read this letter, don't put it down, I need to talk to someone. I should've returned to school, but I signed up for Job Corp and was supposed to leave with the next group. I'm so mixed up. I feel like I'm lost. I was mixed up in this drug deal, but I didn't kill anybody. Please, I need somebody to believe me. I was wrong, but I did not kill anybody.

After six months of correspondence, I decided to take the trip to the prison. I drove an hour and 25 minutes to Waupun from Milwaukee. On the freeway, I wondered how I would react or what to say to a former student who I wanted to see successful. Regrettably, it did not happen that way. Now Elliot was sentenced to life without parole. Whether, he pulled the trigger or not, the law was clear.

Living in poverty never secures the high paid attorneys, even if not guilty. Sometimes being in the wrong place, at the wrong time or worst being with the wrong people can cause problems. Elliot said, he did not kill anybody. The drug dealer was from Chicago and he was the one who fired the shots. I do not know if he was guilty or not, but God arranged this visit. When I arrived at the prison, I did not utter a word for the first 30 minutes, Elliot talked nonstop.

He said, "I stand before you as a guilty man. I'm not worthy of a visit, but you're here, and I'm so grateful that you made the trip! There isn't much hope for me, but maybe, just maybe, I can tell some other boys at the school not to choose the path I took." My heart bled as Elliot spoke. Sadly, he was right. His situation was summed up correctly. There was not much anyone could do, but maybe his story could turn someone's life around.

Occasionally, I would visit Elliot, many days he was fighting discouragement and depression. I understood because I could never imagine being imprisoned for life. "Write a poem, or write a short story," I suggested. Elliot began to write; his stories and poems were shared with our teachers and students at the center. Elliot became hopeful that his writings might deter others from the lure of fast money and empty promises of the streets. In the end, the greatest gift I offered Elliott was hope that his life mattered to others and he could possibly save other young people from a similar fate. The hardest thing to digest was Elliot almost got out. His mother left Chicago to make a better life for family in Milwaukee and it did not work out. She returned to the familiar and the familiar swallowed her son alive.

TOMS
(TIPS ON MOVING STUDENTS)

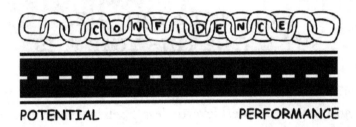

POTENTIAL   PERFORMANCE

- *Safeguard against behaviors that disrupt the learning process*
- *Criminal behavior finds its way into the school don't allow it to overtake you*
- *Teaching can go from classroom to prison walls find lessons to benefit all*

CHAPTER NINE

IT IS NOT ABOUT ME,
BUT MAYBE THIS TIME IT IS

This chapter talks about me, it reflects ending an era and beginning a new one. Nevertheless, I believe it has implications for all educators as well. In most books, there is true confession. As an administrator, I dreamed of all children being successful in life. In a perfect world that would be possible—not in an imperfect one. Still, I longed to see children happy with smiles on their faces when they passed tests, memorized poems, or performed in school programs. The death of a student was the ultimate betrayal of circumstances they did not choose to be born in. I mean tragic deaths, senseless deaths! I remember once reading a quote from Mother Theresa that said, "I know God will not give me anything I can't handle, I just wish He didn't trust me so much."

Like Mother Theresa, God must have thought I could handle this assignment of being trusted with the destiny of children no one else believed in. For me it is mind boggling and humbling. Sometimes I just walked around the school building and questioned my Creator, *Lord, why am I here? What is my purpose?* Then, every time I talked to one of our new students and understood their needs, the answers became clear in my heart. I knew why. A soft inner voice said to me, "Serve My children."

I served at the Assessment Center for five years total through heartbeats (life) and heartaches (death). I witnessed successes through interventions, adjustments and watched students become better. I also watched them become worst. Love and nurturing were the catalysts to conquering academic challenges to transform lives. Passing through Lapham was a huge part of my journey. While working there my space needed to inspire me the second I stepped through my door. Butterflies. I chose beautiful butterflies— my office was loaded with them. I found a way to use butterflies to encourage students, I would tell them—they were in the cocoon stage of life upon entering the center and they could emerge like a magnificent butterfly or die a caterpillar. Butterflies represents life's transformation.

Veteran teacher Francis Gilmore imparted in me that a program was only as strong as its administrator. Her statement had brought a tingling sensation to me— like a shot in the arm because it was true. Students sent to the center were shackled with unimaginable burdens in their lives and needed more help. They were hardened, broken, neglected, and without any tangible hope. She asked me, "How do you stay with such students?" Through God's grace was the only answer I could give. He gave me an abundant amount of grace. The Lord knew I needed it. The gravity of dealing with troubled children labeled as failures tore my heart apart bit by bit. Children sent to Lapham were rejected by society, school and home. Rejection of any kind is life destroying, you hear many so-called experts tell you how to get pass rejection, but sometimes rejection does not get pass you. What do you do then? It lingers like a bad cold. And to rid bad cold you must take care of it until the symptoms disappear, or else it will get worst. I did not want my babies to feel rejected or get worst. Nurturing, love and compassion restores life, it is the antidote. I was determined to show all three.

I am not saying it was always a breeze—I am saying that my heart was committed to the call, God had placed on my life.

The words of teacher James Gauthier, "If the head does not believe in the school; we are lost" echoed those of Mrs. Gilmore. He said to me, "Leadership makes the difference. A school cannot succeed without good leadership." I was left with the decision to figure out some things to produce the best instructional leader possible. Those lasting comments were appreciated. To be effective I had to—learn how not to let pride come in and listen to others. Valuable input was indeed welcome. It is possible to obtain great knowledge, but without the benefit of wisdom. Working with children required both as I reflect on my early days with students who were considered at-risk, difficult or special-needs.

My strength was found in formulating action, while staying encouraged and motivated in light or dark moments. I had my portion of experiences that led me close to the edge. One push came from refereeing a fist fight—not the boys this time, it was the girls. It was a full- blown hair-pulling "title" match. A girl participant in the battle was throwing her balled fist wildly in the air. I recognized her, it was Dana, the student I was mentoring. Outside the line of fire, I was positioned to separate everyone involved. However, the next punch thrown hit me with such force, it knocked me down to my knees. Dana knocked the wind out of me. Once this skirmish was over I regained composure and retreated down the stairs, hurt, injured and disgusted for several reasons. The betrayal I felt.

In my office, I took a few minutes to process what just happened and checked for any signs of physical injuries. Confused over this, the same old question resurfaced again, "Why am I here in this crazy job?" I had thoughts of leaving because there was not enough pay for me to stay. Never in my lifetime I have been knocked down to my knees before by anyone. What a rude awakening, here I work day and night, and this is what I get. "No. I am leaving!"

Dana came to see me—I refused to see her. Yes, I was hotter than July. Apparently, someone told her that she punched me.

Reluctantly, I finally agreed to see her. She apologized and asked for my forgiveness. While in my office she started to cry crocodile tears. I could tell they were genuine and her heart was breaking. I walked over to Dana with an embrace to let her know—she was forgiven.

My state of mind required me to regroup and pray to my Creator, He then spoke to my spirit and told me, "Unto whom much is given, much is required" My heart spoke back, *I refuse to be angry with this child and Lord, thank You for keeping me safe. Now direct me to properly instruct the children and staff to prevent this from happening again.* I talked to God sometimes with my heart as though speaking words. The remaining three years was not trouble free, but I was never assaulted again.

If it sounds like missed opportunities were taken personally because I did. It had to be personal for me to effectively change lives at an alternative school. I could not afford to detach or be indifference, the stakes were too high. Besides unconcern for their well- being was what placed students there in the first place. For me, it became more than a job, it became a mission. Making a difference for students was my priority and I emphasized this to students until it was a priority to them. They were looking for words with actions, not action- less words. No one can give their all unless it is made personal.

Days were long and sometimes the nights were longer. I did not stop with a punch of the timeclock. Yet, I had a life too. My children were young, and they needed nurturing and love like most of my students were missing. I had to fulfill other obligations and I did everything to the best of my [natural] ability. When you are called by God— most times— you must go beyond normal lengths— when others who are doing the same thing— can simply lay it down at the end of their shift. Drive is placed in the heart, when this happens you put your mind in gear and move forward to do the work. This is what I had to do.

Roughly 900 days of my life was devoted to Lapham Assessment Center without one single regret. Educators are underpaid and overworked—no one can argue that—if the passion is true, we still do it. The rewards are far greater than the pay. Although, states, local cities and districts need to invest more in education, it will not stop the determined teacher on assignment from doing the job. I had a front row seat and watched the lives of children born into poverty, drug infested neighborhoods, gangs, abandonment and it gave me a more compassionate heart with an expanded perspective on how to educate them. The streets did not love them back and the streets were choking the life out of its most vulnerable citizens (children). Society was very unkind to them and today it still is. I did not like what was placed before my eyes. Oftentimes I would go to bed with the world's weight on my mind. I could not fix everything, but I would at least try to fix what the Lord gave me. I had successes and failures to teach me how to succeed more. The paradigm needed to shift in a new direction of hope.

African American [poor] children frequently received the short end of the stick inside a system purposely designed to limit their capability or eliminate them period. That bothered me. The boys had it harder than girls with similarities that mirrored the days of slavery. In every grade starting from kindergarten to 12th grade, the boys failed the most. The cycle of the break-away fathers continued from past generations— even today. All of this took a toll on my heart because I knew education would help in some way. Everyone is not college bound for many different reasons, but a basic quality education is owed to every child in this country, and I hold firm to this belief. There is an old cliché *you pay for what you don't know*, a relevant truth on so many levels, it is hard to function in a world without knowledge, common sense or wisdom. All children are precious no matter what circumstances surrounds their lives. Pushing them to their full potential was my goal; I wanted them so desperately to defy the odds within a school system that was not doing enough to provide a decent education and there are countless studies to support what I am saying. Soon, I grew weary of seeing African American children at risk and no one taking a risk— and from that Ceria M. Travis Academy was birthed.

TOMS
(TIPS ON MOVING STUDENTS)

POTENTIAL   PERFORMANCE

- *Never imagined education would encapsulate my heart like it did*
- *Trust the process and grow exponentially from it*
- *Through the peaks and valleys of the journey, stay encouraged*

CHAPTER TEN

THE TRUMPET SOUNDED

Leaving Lapham Park Assessment Center was bittersweet and on to my [final] destination with MPS I moved to Lincoln Middle School of the Arts. My mother had been deceased for ten years I could still hear her profound words whispering in my ears. When I was growing up she would say often, "We have got to do something with our boys if we are going to save the African American families!" I decided to start a school that offered something a little different and go the extra mile to serve boys who were lost. The idea had germinated in my mind and swelled up in my spirit for several years.

Education had its hooks in me, it was 1995 almost 20 years after my career began. I loved being around the children and wanted to give more. The process of starting a school began and I called Dr. Howard Fuller, who was the superintendent at MPS during that time and informed him of my interest in launching a school—perhaps a charter one.

Lamenting to him that my heart burned like *fire* to reach young boys in the community who were falling through the cracks. Every time I picked up the newspaper, the dropout and suspension rate spiraled higher among African American boys and the trumpet needed to be sounded. These young boys just were not doing well in the schools. The move was bold because I was employed by MPS and could have jeopardized my position. The time had come — I just had to do it.

The year before Travis Academy was started, I had a noble idea. I decided to run an intensive summer program with some of the boys from Lincoln Middle School to put my theory to test. My son Terrance helped me with the preparation. It was called *The Summer Behavior Improvement Program.* Approximately 20 boys were involved. At the end, they achieved slightly more than modicum of success, but better than nothing— and enough to let me know the concept held promise, and time to do more. My deep faith in God helped me to walk in unfamiliar territory, He ordered my steps and showed me to watch each one.

Honestly, I was afraid. I did not know all the business mechanics necessary to start the school; however, I was resourceful and a good educator. I came from Mississippi and learned how to make something out of nothing. The Lord was with me and I needed His reassurance every waking day of my life. Establishing a choice school took courage and like Gideon in the bible I fought with little. Because I was not quite ready to start I stayed at Lincoln Middle School for another year and a half. During my stint there, it gave me a chance to reflect on many valuable moments, and how God had always brought me through tougher times. He did not leave me, nor forsake me— this still rings true. When the timing was right, He impressed upon me to move on. God kept nudging and poking until my spirit knew.

It is easier for people to travel a familiar road, than the road less traveled. I had reached its proverbial fork. I needed more confirmation from God. He instructed me to seek counsel and obtain reinforcements. The summer of 1996, I requested an audience before Pastor Julius Malone and the Elder Board at New Testament Church. I shared the vision God gave me and how I felt lead to establish a private school for boys. I was looking for spiritual insight and direction, not money— yet they agreed to give me a monthly stipend and included me as part of the mission's outreach program.

Pastor Malone said something that I shall never forget, *"Dorothy if God is God, then just do it!"* After that meeting, I was fired up and ready to go. The deep concern about helping boys had been implanted by my mother's words and deeds. As my tribute to her, the school was named Ceria M. Travis Academy in her honor.

The idea of a boys' school was on its way to reality. I believe people are placed here for divine purpose given to them by God. Most of my life I worked in church without a specific ministry. What I mean is that I taught Sunday school, lead youth groups and women's ministries but now I would hang my hat in education building a legacy to please God.

My daughter, Wilnekia and I received invitations to Memphis, Tennessee where she sang at a citywide youth rally sponsored by motivational speaker Joseph Jennings. Something extraordinary happened to me that night. After the assembly was over; the youth wanted to stay longer. The principal gave permission to students who wanted to remain in the auditorium for a more personal conversation with Mr. Jennings. A heavy atmosphere of oppression and pain still lingered over the auditorium that needed to be lifted. Those hurting and damaged children needed someone to listen to them. Mr. Jennings broke the students into small groups and several helpers who participated in the rally served as group leaders. There was an overflow of children and Mr. Jennings approached me to asked if I would take a group.

My group had nearly 50 children, I collected them and headed to the stage. Then, God's spirit led me to close the curtains for privacy, suddenly the children began to talk. They were between 14-16 years old and began to open the waterfall of their hearts.

They talked about being cold in the winter time because they were prohibited from entering their home after school. If the mother was entertaining male clients, they had to wait outside until customers left. Girls attested to tragic incidents of regularly being sexually abused by male friends of their mothers. Even more tragic was that the mothers did not realize what was happening or did not care. They complained their parents took grocery money and bought drugs, instead of food and clothes. Boys stated some of them were victimized by older brothers and forced to distribute drugs or get beaten. One child after another poured out to me.

Finally, I told them that there was strength in numbers. I stressed they were not alone and to lean on each other for help and support. The moment was special. Then, I asked them to tightly hold hands to form a circle; the Holy Spirit began to move.

Mindful of the school setting, I declared in obedience to God "Memphis schools did not hire me, and Memphis schools cannot fire me. I am going to tell you about somebody who will be your friend long after I am gone. I am going to tell you about someone who wants to love you and save you, with an incredible almighty power. Let me tell you about Jesus Christ." Next I prayed, and we prayed and prayed. This night was a turning point in my life. The following day on my way back to Milwaukee, I had a "spiritual" revelation to give the gospel of Jesus Christ to children. Yes, I had been called to teach and preach. This mission of starting a school with disadvantaged students that God was leading me to do became clearer.

The school would have started in September, however I kept telling myself to make one more check because I had no idea where my income was coming from once I resigned. Over the summer my office was bare. Previous years I always recycled old home decorations to make my office comfortable and welcoming. Not this time. I knew the spirit of God had spoken to me and I was not supposed to be there. There was not much time left before my official departure.

Near the end, a sixth-grade teacher burst into my office enraged about an unruly student. She wanted this child suspended going on and on. Abruptly, in mid-sentence she noticed the sparsely decorated room. With a frown on her face, she wanted to know what was wrong with my office. I simply smiled. I did not know how to tell her I leaving soon to start a school. The mission was understood, but it took a few more months to officially resign.

After my resignation, I felt free to walk in the steps ordered by God. I never told anyone what had transpired with the meeting with Pastor Malone or the elders in August 1996; no one knew of any timeline.

I was leaving church on an August night and headed upstairs where Betty Allen was cleaning the building. She knew only the Pastor and elders were supposed to be there, which prompted her question "What you are doing here tonight, Dorothy?" I told her we had discussed starting a school for at risk boys. A great big smile came across her face, she expressed her interest because her grandson needed a school. Also, she inquired about which grades would be taught. I informed her sixth through eighth grades; immediately, she requested the first application. Although, I did not have application form developed, I promised to send it and rushed home to create one for Betty to fill out. She completed the first application promptly and returned it to me. This divine encounter was nothing less than confirmation from God. When September rolled around the school was not operational. I called to let Betty know about the delay and told her when the doors opened, she would be the first to know.

Unable to physically pull myself away from Lincoln Middle School, my hesitancy centered around concerns of being financially destitute. A *real* fear that held me back. Two months later Betty called me at Lincoln. She asked, "Dorothy, when are you going to start that school? My grandson is in trouble and has been kicked out of school again." She was the messenger God used to light flames under my feet. This was Him reinforcing the needs I had to meet. I promised Betty the school would open after Thanksgiving—which fell on December 2nd, the following Monday after the holiday. With a little push from Betty I was reminded there was one student ready to go. Things began to come together, the course I was pursuing felt good— especially my walk by faith with the Lord.

Around lunchtime I decided to leave school in search for a place to begin a new school. I ended up on North Avenue driving up and down the street asking the Lord to direct me to the *right* building. Then, my eyes fell on the corner of 47th and North Avenue. There was a perfect little building for lease. I wrote the number down to call after lunch.

After calling the owner, he agreed to meet after school. I kept wondering what was the price, since I had no budget or money. But I knew it was time to trust God for the school. Once I arrived the location, I told the Lord about my lack of finances and asked Him what should I pay for this building? Instantly, a dollar amount popped up in my spirit. The owner was a very pleasant gentleman showed me the entire space. It was perfect with four small classrooms, reception area, large office, lunch area and restrooms. I asked about the cost, the owner replied, "It's $600 a month." I said to myself, *Oh no that is not the amount in my spirit*. Without any coaxing he said, "If you pay in advance, it will be $500 a month." The exact amount and I gladly took it. My last semester needed to be finished at Lincoln, when the concern for teachers occurred to me. I called my nephew, Travis McGlothian, who was a senior at the University of Wisconsin – Milwaukee. Travis had always been a highly intelligent young man, he attended Golda Meir, Morse Middle School and Riverside University High School. I knew that he would be instrumental in imparting great knowledge into the children. I asked him if he was interested in a part-time job; he said yes! Travis became the first teacher at our school. Mr. John Williams was the Dean of Men and the secretary was a volunteer, we were on our way to opening our first day of school. At the semester's ending, I took a bold step and resigned from the Milwaukee Public Schools in January of 1997. My resignation shocked many people, in fact it shocked most people. When the Milwaukee Public Schools' Central Administration got wind of my plans to leave, that office summoned me to a meeting at its Central Office. Four people were present at this exit conference to inquire about the reasons for my departure. They asked if I enjoyed my job and stated the district really wanted me to help further develop Lincoln. The committee members interrogated me. I told them there was nothing wrong, it was time to move on and do what I believed God had instructed me to do. One asked me that magical question, "How are you going to fund your school?" Looking straight in their eyes I confessed, "I am not sure, but I know it is something that I simply have to do." Everyone's head was turning and their eyes flashing back and forth with quizzical expressions of disbelief. The look on their faces gave me the impression their minds were saying, *Oh my goodness, we know this intelligent woman is not going to make such a foolish mistake.* I did not care what they thought, and that conversation concluded with well wishes.

Walking down the corridor I felt their eyes following me, so I mustered all of my confidence with until I faded out of sight, pleading to the Lord, *Dear God, do not let me stumble now. All I have is You. If I could ask anything, I would ask to let Your glory shine through.* With the resignation accepted this faith walk became more real.

TOMS
(TIPS ON MOVING STUDENTS)

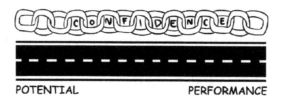

POTENTIAL   PERFORMANCE

- *Step on out into the deep. Dreams need to be fulfilled*
- *Fear is a reality when one door is closed but another one is opening*
- *Turning points come in our lives for a reason, follow the leading*

PART TWO

CHAPTER ELEVEN

STEPPING OUT ON FAITH

December 2, 1996 was a cool Monday morning. The first day at Ceria M. Travis Academy was filled with excitement and in my hand, were shiny new keys. Durrell Miller was the [first] sixth grade student to arrive through the doors. In our God directed building, my mini staff was in place. Durrell's academics began with one on one instruction from his teacher, Mr. McGlothian. We engaged him with the day to day operations as the incentive, which resulted with completion of his work. He loved the attention! The first week Durrell's assignment was to help set up equipment, including the fax machine. He was a chatterbox who loved to talk and would often serve as our student receptionist, answering phones in the afternoons. By week two, our enrollment doubled. We welcomed another student named Michael Mayo, Jr. to the seventh grade. Now, we had two students. Quickly, word traveled in the community that an all boys' school had started. The referrals poured in from both public and private schools. Our enrollment had increased to 17 students by first semester's end in January. Between both schools, I still needed to finalize things at Lincoln to finish out my last days. My conversation with the principal and teachers can be summed up this way. They told me how sorry they were to see me leave but if I must go take Fred, Michael and Robert (sixth graders with behavior problems) with me. The boys' parents agreed to transfer all three of them to Travis Academy.

Enrolled students paid a small tuition, brought their lunch and transportation was the responsibility of parents. The first year I could see changes in the boys. They were beginning to do more classwork than ever before. In fact, Fred commented that he had never worked this hard at school. My response was, "I know and that is why we have Travis Academy." Other boys came to us during this period as the student population grew. One student named Calvin stood out. He was such a smart young man, but he could not stop talking. We spent a month trying to redirect his conversation and set up a behavior modification program for him. Calvin loved to swim, and we had several swimming trips planned. His permission to go swimming was contingent on him keeping quiet during instructional time. Initially, the teacher made him aware of his actions hourly. Once his focus increased it changed to every two hours. And finally, the reminders were at the end of each day. Calvin learned to change his negative behavior from talking too much with swimming trips as his reward.

The word continued to spread that our school was open. Also, we accepted boys who had problems in their regular session. Enrollment was on the rise and I needed more space, the apartment on the second floor of our building became available and we transformed it into a classroom. Teacher by teacher our staff was growing, I hired another part time teacher, Mr. Garnell Murray who taught our boys math.

Families of students arrived at Travis Academy. Brothers and extended relatives that came from the same household. We had one family with two boys Evan and Ian. Evan was the sixth grader and Ian was seventh grader. These boys needed a smaller setting, their mother could not pay tuition and their enrollment; the cost was waived. Often, I brought lunch for them, because the mother simply could not afford to. They came to school wearing dirty clothes and it was evident they had not bathe. Evan and Ian's confidence were extremely low, their aggression high and they would fight with the drop of a hat. They never brought school supplies and confrontations with other students were almost daily. We worked tirelessly for their behavior to change.

Our first year, we acquired a 15 passenger van to assist parents with transportation needs. The neighborhoods where our students lived were disadvantaged— and high crime was the norm. Some mornings I would drive to pick up students. On one stop, I beeped the horn, no one came out. Fearlessly or foolishly I got out. Three people were going to the side of the house while I was going to the front. Then, I saw them at the window exchanging money for what appeared to be drugs. My initial thought was these young men are selling drugs out of their mother's home. But when I got closer to the window, it was not the young men, but their mother. Witnessing this gave me an appreciation for what my boys were going through. I returned to the van to wait a few minutes, the boys finally came out. Shockingly, one of them told me not to knock on the door because their grandmother sleeps in the front room with a gun, and they did not want her to shoot me. Well, I did not want her to shoot me either! The incident caused safety concerns and all van drivers were advised not go to the door, just sound the horn.

Once we made it to school, I talked to the boys about different lifestyles. I wanted them to understand sometimes you cannot control what goes on in your house, but education could lead you to a better life. They had so many unmet needs, I wanted to help them. Members from my church was willing to donate clothes and one member agreed to expose them to youth activities on the weekend. Children do not choose their parents and [they] should not have to feel guilty or insignificant for their parents' shortcomings or poor choices. God will substitute other people to appreciate, nurture and educate them. I believe Travis Academy was chosen for that reason.

Parents were pleased with the progress of their boys, however paying tuition was a strain on the family's budget. We needed school materials to complete the upcoming classroom lessons. I decided to take the money from my retirement fund to use to complete our school year. Also, we still received monthly donations from the church under their mission's program. Overjoyed to receive any help from God. With limited funds, we had to do something fast. The state offered a school voucher program; I began to do research for our school to become part of the Milwaukee Parental Choice Program. Somewhat familiar with a few aspects of the program from attending several meetings, I completed "An Intent to Participate" with the Department of Public Instruction. By God's grace our school became eligible to receive funds for the 1997-1998 school year. Thirty boys enrolled with their education cost paid for without financial burden to parents. Also, we enrolled in the state offered nutrition program for free or reduced lunch.

What our boy's academy stood for garnered the attention of Bill Taylor, a reporter from *Positively Milwaukee*. Our story needed to be told. The free publicity extended our reach in the community. From our story airing locally the Milwaukee Area Technical College called to donate 15 computers because of their generosity, we added computer classes to the curriculum. This news made the boys excited and they were jumping up and down, "high fiving" each other.

Applications poured in. The staff spent all summer long making class assignments and adjustments to our small classrooms. Our enrollment rose to upwards of 50 and 60 boys in September. We had to search for new teachers and gather new materials geared toward the "at risk" student to stay well informed.

Before school started in the fall, I received a call from a national television station from New York City. The person on the phone's other end said to me, "As school is about to begin, we know that troublesome students can cause schools great stress. Most schools are not looking forward to having disruptive students return. We understand that you have a school for disruptive boys. And how do you feel about them returning to school?"

I did not appreciate her uncompassionate remarks about students she had never met or knew their life circumstances, this angered me. "I am looking forward to it", I said. But still, I needed to share something with her. I told her our academy had some bright young men and I was very excited to see them, because it gave me a chance to help them learn and grow. Her next interview question troubled me more, "Aren't you fearful of them?" There was silence.

"Fearful of what?" I said. "These are precious students looking for adults to help teach and shape their lives into positive individuals. This is a great time to be in education and I would not have it any other way. All my life's work has been with troublesome students and I have seen greatness come out of them." This answered her questions.

The interview lasted about 15 more minutes and I defended the potential in boys with bad behavior. Her voice paused. "Just one moment," she left the phone. I waited wondering, what question was next. She returned to the phone, "We'd like to fly a crew out there to your school on the opening day." Her request was granted. I told her we would love that. The station sent a crew and spent the entire morning with us. Later, Travis Academy's special aired on national television. It was a wonderful experience, first we had local coverage then graduated [no pun intended] to national television and this brought several supporters to our school to assist us.

Initially, we were only taking students in sixth and seventh grades. The second year a principal with a troublesome teen called to see if he could transfer to our school. We understood our students were not the best behaved group, but this eighth grader named Shawn smoked cigarettes. On one occasion, Mr. McGlothian had students outside for a science project, Shawn cajoled two other boys to far side of the building to smoke a cigarette. Mr. McGlothian observed them and asked him to stop, but he refused. He was asked to leave the premises if he was not going to stop smoking, and his mother was notified of the situation. Shawn made matters worse and cursed out the teacher in front of everyone. As students returned to the building, Shawn was not allowed to re-enter. It was amazing how other students identified and felt sorry for him when he was not allowed back to class. To deescalate this volatile situation, Mr. McGlothian went back outside and escorted him to the bus stop. Once he returned to the classroom, he told students that he realized teenagers smoked, but at Travis Academy that behavior was not tolerated, and he talked more about smoking and their health.

In the middle of Mr. McGlothian's lecture to students, he noticed one student had left the classroom to unlock the door to let Shawn back inside the building. Again, he came in cursing and fussing to the point his parents were called again about him not leaving school property. The mother was informed that Shawn would receive a Disciplinary Time Out (DTO) for two days unless he followed our school rules. I never liked to use the word suspension because it had more of a negative stigma attached. His mother called and relayed something good was happening at our school and her son wanted to be there. Shawn returned the next day and responded well to school guidelines. He loved math and finished top of his class. Maybe it was not the last time Shawn smoked a cigarette, but it was the last time he smoked at Travis Academy.

Our teachers would deal with a variety of negative behaviors, but they had learned that a student's personal situation cannot lower their classrooms expectations. Our school was new, and we were empathetic to the plight of our young [inner] city males; our job was to expose better options, teach the value of their lives and give hope for the future. This year would end with an enrollment of 65 boys. It was clear we had outgrown our space and needed a new home of our own.

TOMS
(TIPS ON MOVING STUDENTS)

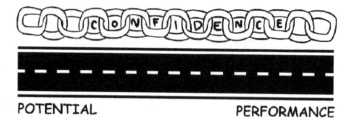

POTENTIAL   **PERFORMANCE**

- *Classroom expectations must not be lowered, just modified*
- *Understand the connect that students have with each other*
- *Value parents, they echo the journey; pitch in financially*

CHAPTER TWELVE

A PLACE OF OUR OWN

We were bursting at the seams on North Avenue. Betty Allen to the rescue, again! During a parent meeting Betty announced, "I think I found a larger building." The Hillside Boys and Girls Club was leasing some space during the day. They had a beautiful building on 623 W. Cherry Street. We met with the director and he allowed us to lease the space. The club's activities started after our regular Monday through Friday school hours, which ended at 4:00 PM. This place had an art room, game room and full- sized gym. The boys could get lost in its enormous size and classrooms were set up in certain sections of the building. Amenities were available for the boys to enjoy. In the afternoon when the boys finished their core academics they participated in Physical Education, which they loved.

Each day sparked new challenges, I had a mother who came to our academy with four boys. Every single one had been kicked out of regular school. My heart ached for all involved and I wondered what was going on in the lives of these boys. We agreed to take them, shortly after a team meeting was held to discuss their needs, understand some things and find out who they were. These boys were placed in four different classrooms and teachers had plans ready. The first 30 days were rough, but teachers were patient— and kept working with the boys until finally we could see a small measurable difference. We used behavioral modification techniques to give consequences for negative actions the moment it started and I liked what our teachers had accomplished. The boys talked a lot about their home life; the father was absent and not one of them liked the mother's live in boyfriend. Personal discussions were kept confidential unless abuse or neglect occurred. We encouraged counseling for families to gain perspective and possible resolutions for relationship issues. I invited the boys' mother to come in and review progress reports. She could not believe that her boys completed assignments and passed their tests. I expressed to her it appeared that there were no limits set at home. When asked, she admitted they were left alone and I suggested more supervision. We went over our structured classroom setting and rewards program. Also, I suggested she ask for a doctor's referral to see a counselor or therapist.

It is not easy to recommend some things to parents that they should do to improve their children's behavior. Educators need to know deep in their hearts that they want to serve and help children. If parents think otherwise, then trust becomes non-existent. Our teachers were instructed to call student's home a minimum of once a month to establish a bond between home and school. Trust building was needed on all sides. The bible tells us in Proverbs 22:6 *To train up a child in the way that he should go and when he is old he will not depart from it.* Structure begins in the home, but if the home is negligent, the school is left with picking up the broken pieces. I am not saying it is right or fair because God gives children to parents, however sometimes the school must serve in the parents' stead. I believe if a school can serve a need, then that school must do so.

We Challenge the Challenged

For example, we wanted to serve a different type of need, a student named Elijah, who was considered mentally challenged. His parents were unhappy with his school setting. They approached Travis Academy about placement. We were a school for at- risk students, not necessarily *Special Education* children with low functioning abilities, but we did not discriminate either. I wondered if we were a match for this student, based on his criteria. The parents were concerned for Elijah's well -being and did not like the unfriendly treatment from other students who laughed at him. They felt he might adjust to a smaller setting. We agreed to place him on a trial basis. For starters, Elijah's awkward demeanor and lack of social skills made it difficult for him to fit in, even at Travis Academy. Yet, we were determined to work with him and his parents. We took opportunities to teach students that everyone is different, and everyone is a valuable human being. Honestly, we did not know if Elijah was going to make it in our setting. However, his parents noticed a difference. His self- confidence level changed, he bonded with classmates and participated in more school activities— by year's end he was *one of the guys.*

Elijah was indeed different, and he accepted it. His parents saw the benefit of a smaller class size and nurturing environment and praised the staff for their efforts. Parents need to know no matter where they send their children, just make sure the education is measured by nurturing and love in academics and behavior, and grow the same standards as any other child, even if they attended an Ivy League School. I used to say to the students at Travis Academy, "Let's make this like an all- boys Ivy League School here in the Midwest." The first year at Hillside we had 100 boys running around and playing doing what little boys do. Regrettably, the Hillside Boys and Girls Club decided not to renew our lease for a second year. I believed God that we would find a nice building by September. To keep the academics going during summer break we decided to have a *Reading Enrichment Program*. We needed space for that too, one of the area's leaders Bishop William Strong, offered his church basement and we held the program at Greater New Bethel Full Gospel Baptist Church.

September rolled in quicker than expected. Still no building, the search for another location was on again. I was driving around and saw a [corner] building on 28th Street and Wisconsin Avenue for lease. I met the building manager and found out the rent was too high. I asked the manager to talk with the owner and proposed a low rent that would increase once enrollment was up. It took nearly four weeks to come up with agreement and I was pleased with the outcome. During my morning meditation, I thanked God for His mercy and favor with renting the building. Then the thought came, *If you can believe God to rent the building, you can believe God to purchase the building.* I asked the manager to contact the owner about the building's purchase. I could visualize the look on the manager's face saying, "Lady you barely have enough money to pay rent, how are you going to buy it?" Nevertheless, he took my request to the owner. Two days later, he said the owner wants to talk about selling the building. The asking price was too expensive, and the owner would not negotiate a lower amount. It turned out that the second- floor tenants Well Baby Clinic, lost their grant and had to move out. Due to these unexpected turn of events, I called my attorney, Mike Zeka, and he advised it was to my advantage to bid because an empty building is worth a lot less than a full one. We purchased our building considerably lower than the asking price.

We settled into our new surroundings. The staff and student population grew large enough to start a sports program. Academic standards were made high and no students could play sports if they did not have good grades and good attendance. Adding sports to the curriculum motivated the boys; we taught the importance of camaraderie, team work and commitment, it somehow fulfilled a void and made them dream. The best part was when they won their first championship game!

Until High School Do We Part

The boys had mixed emotions of joy and sadness. The joy came from seeing more academic possibilities—sadness as they became closer to completion of eighth grade, which meant promotion to high school. The goal of Travis Academy was to propel at risk middle school boys onward and develop young men to reach further than their circumstances. The first three years were good, but parting was always difficult.

More students applied, and transportation needed to be expanded to help parents get children to school. We shopped around for a larger 70 passenger bus. It turns out the cost was too expensive, or it was in poor condition. A member from our Board of Directors worked for a transportation company. He called me excited and said, "You aren't going to believe this. The company has just received a bus with low miles, it meets Wisconsin's specifications, it's nearly new and the price is right. It's yours if you want it." God had worked out another miracle. Good news for both parents and students alike, just in time because a family called and asked about transportation. An immediate need was met.

The Struggle is Real

In this case, this mother was referred to us because her son was failing all his classes in a northwestern school system. Stunned, I asked her, "Did you name a northwestern school system?" At the time, it was nearly an all- white school district. The mother explained that her son had attended there from kindergarten to eighth grade. Now, he hated school and refused to go. I had no words. But I did have questions. "Ma'am is your son behind in his academics, considered a disruptive troublemaker or suspended from school?" Her response was no.

I went on to tell her "Ma'am, I do not think your son is a match for our school. We have children who struggle with academic success." Her son did not fit out criteria for enrollment. She cried out. "But my friends at New Testament Church told me you could help, we don't know what to do. Help me!" I could hear her desperation and agreed to interview them. At the meeting, the son came off a little shy. Basically, he attended a school system that welcomed him from kindergarten through fourth grade. In his words, then the mistreatment started in the fifth grade. My heart went out to him. I was familiar with this type of problem, an African American student attending an all-white school district. At first, they see a cute little boy, up until about fourth grade. Then, comes discrimination and the child becomes ostracized and unwelcomed in their world. This rejection took a toll on him—he felt worthless. I explained to his mother in detail about the type of students we had at Travis Academy, but with God's grace we would try to work with her son. It was tricky putting a non- risk student in the middle of at risk students with juvenile records. Our new student Aaron came to school and the other boys began to see his academic skills. They were asking him for classroom help and valued his contribution to the classroom. It was not long before they encouraged and let him know how smart he was.

Soon Aaron's countenance changed, his self-esteem improved. He offered academic leadership to students and they offered sports leadership to him. I could not believe it, the boys were exchanging their strengths and working together. I remember hearing one of the boys talking to him, "Say man, you don't have any problems compared to us. You have a mom and dad, they both have jobs. You have a house that you own. Man, that's no trouble. We move every other month if my mom can't pay the rent and sometimes we don't have food to eat. I got a reason to be sad and not come to school, you don't."

What that student said was true, although Aaron had social and economic advantages the other boys did not have, he was still African American, which caused problems for Aaron when it should not have. He finished eighth grade with a new- found energy ready to go to high school. Aaron was not your typical at-risk student, but it did not mean he was risk-free.

Our philosophy was to strengthened young boys and mold them to become community leaders or activists. It was our job to develop their sense of confidence, culture and character that would prevent any other race from tearing them down.

The way we operated started to go in a different direction, after accepting Aaron I guess you would say opened the door beyond our criteria. Our open door was right across the street from Wisconsin Avenue Elementary school and a new relationship was established with them. They heard about our work with at risk boys, it was not long before they sent troubled students over from their school. We went from serving sixth through eighth grades to serving fourth and fifth grades. My greatest shock came when the school's psychologist walked a third grader over to our building to seek help. This forced us to reevaluate our mission. I knew our children in middle school around the country were considered out of control, but what was happening in the lower graders?

I talked to our Board of Directors and we decided to include third graders. Serving eight-year-old students brought out the creativity in our teachers because Travis Academy appealed to special types of families. Reaching young student not doing well in traditional schools was our priority. I spoke with a parent who signed up her child; her son Nate was very smart, but a little hyper. She said his previous school called her daily and she missed work, she needed a school that could handle her child properly. What she failed to disclose was Nate cussed and fought teachers. Nor did we know he was beating up other children and running around destroying property.

Mr. McGlothian was the Assistant Principal and Nate was sent to his office daily. Did I mention he was in the second grade? I took in account the problems the mother had on her new job and opted not to call her. Mr. McGlothian searched for creative ways to curb his behavior. Nate really loved wrestling— I had an idea.

He brought a wrestling man action figure every day and would not allow anyone to touch it. The action figure was the wrestler Bautista! Mr. McGlothian took Bautista and used him to talk to the Nate. Mr. McGlothian put the toy on his chest and changed his voice and would say things like, "If you don't sit down and listen to your teacher, I'll never be able to come back to you." In the beginning, the other students laughed, but soon they participated and would say, "You better sit down, he's going to take Bautista." When Nate concentrated on his work (thanks to Bautista), he did great! In fact, he wrote a speech for the Martin Luther King Speech Writing contest and ended up being a finalist.

Girls Came into Our World

Travis Academy made changes to accommodate more young boys who were getting lost in an educational system that labeled and rejected them. Nonetheless, we were soon faced with a new dilemma when one of our parents called us about enrollment for her daughter. The reason we had an all-boys academy was because African American boys received harsher treatment in society than girls. Little did we know we were about to accept our first girl named Ashley. Ashley had four brothers who already attended Travis Academy. She was kicked out of her middle school and mother said, "I got 11 children, 10 boys and one girl. Ashley can handle being around boys. I want her to attend Travis Academy." Girls were finally admitted to Travis Academy.

As the school year progressed, our lives became more complicated, because I received phone calls from several principals telling me the eighth graders who completed our program with honors—experienced problems in a larger setting. Some of the principals asked me to consider starting a high school. I banished that thought. High School is a different kind of curriculum and it requires more. Parents asked us to start a high school too, they were willing to wait while we prepared for expansion because their suspended children were at home doing nothing. With our backs against the wall, the plans to start a high school were underway.

TOMS
(TIPS ON MOVING STUDENTS)

POTENTIAL   PERFORMANCE

- *Allow relationships to triumph over disabilities or obstacles*
- *Phone calls to parents with positive news increase trust and hope*
- *Reevaluation is constant; plans are often interrupted with new ones*

CHAPTER THIRTEEN

THE HIGH SCHOOL ROAD

Our high program opened with 50 students marching through our doors. It did not take long to see that high school brought its own set of problems totally different from middle school. We needed clear separation between the two programs. Strategically, we placed our elementary and middle schools on the first floor and the high school on the second floor. It was a practical plan, however, we were unsuccessful in keeping students separated at dismissal. The middle school girls were giving their phone numbers to high school boys. We had to put a screeching halt to that behavior and moved with a sense of urgency for a solution. Another building was needed to house our high school program. The Wisconsin African American Women's Center became home to our first high school program. This move solved the problem. This separate environment allowed each staff to concentrate on the needs of their student population. Who would be the leader of this new high school program located at the Women's Center? My daughter who works in education Ms. Wilnekia Brinson (Green) served as the middle school's Guidance Director and she said, "I can be the administrator of the high school program." We hired a group of teachers for core subjects to advance the agenda. The high school students immediately transferred over to the center, but we were still swamped with new applications.

Marie was the first new student to arrive at the Women's Center. She was the mother of a toddler son and pregnant with her second child. A neighbor told her to come to Travis Academy High School for help. She needed six credits to graduate and according to Marie nobody would help. Unfortunately, her son was sick a lot and caused poor attendance that was why other schools dropped her. Ms. Brinson connected her with social services—so she could get assistance with child care. They also talked about a home study program before the new baby's arrival. Seven months pregnant Marie came to school every day, her English teacher, Mr. Marshall Martin tutored her in reading and helped with her social studies project. Marie expressed it had been a long while since she felt like someone cared about her. Her mother passed away two years earlier and her two brothers were incarcerated. "I got an aunt somewhere in the city, but she's an alcoholic, I never spent much time with her," she said. Marie was living with her boyfriend; they both worked evening part time jobs. We had to come up with a feasible plan for her life, it took a few months and the vocational staff really worked to help her. Even after she went on maternity leave for six weeks, the staff took school work to her and picked up the completed assignments. When Marie went to the hospital, someone broke in her house and stole the new baby's items. The kindness of others and our staff helped to replenish her baby supplies. Marie told us before Travis Academy High School— she would have given up and stopped coming to school. Despite her challenges, Marie graduated on time. A positive life change happened for Marie through our program. One hundred students were in the high school program with numbers increasing each year.

We dealt with a very difficult student population —our primary focus was to help them graduate from high school with a diploma, also find employment. When the news spread about Travis

Academy's Vocational High School's program, drop-out students from across the city were returning to school after a two or three years hiatus. They were sitting at home watching television and often getting into trouble. "How can you be out of school for two years?", I asked. One student told me, *no one cared*, which confirmed what other students said. This student took a brave step and decided to return, even with the discouragement from his friends.

Our main priority was basic academic classes and employment, because employment brought money to help them survive. Most job opportunities came from the food industry. In a short time, some of our students were promoted to day shift and night shift leaders. Some were promoted to assistant managers. We placed our students in a variety of jobs throughout the city. The area's International House of Pancakes (IHOP) called to ask us if we had any students available to fill waitress and waiter positions.

The owners Fred and Marion Jones were known as excellent entrepreneurs in the area; our *Vocational Training Specialist* instituted a special program to train students on how to interview for food services positions. The students were pushed to learn interviewing techniques six weeks before their actual interview. This practice worked so well everyone who interviewed received employment. The high school program had two components— vocational and academics. This vocational model allowed students to have academic classes and receive credits for working.

We had probation officers and social workers seeking out our program. One social worker explained there were over 4,000 teenagers not enrolled in any high school that year and it was getting harder and harder to get them to attend. Social workers often searched for schools with unique programs to help students get back into school. Community leaders got on board to also enroll students in our program.

Trying Hard Not to Quit

A church minister brought Darren to our program as an eleventh grader. He was already 19 years old. He wore dirty clothes and looked unkempt. When Darren received homework assignments, he never completed them. Many teachers attempted to help him during the day, but Darren made this odd request to stay late to complete his work. In a staff meeting, a teacher raised concern about Darren being hungry. Other teachers spoke up with the same concern. He asked the staff for money and on several occasions they would give it to him without the principal's knowledge. The math teacher, Ms. Sheila Sykes, decided to investigate, she discovered Darren's grandmother passed away, and he had no place to live. His mother who was not supportive suggested he find for an apartment to rent. Darren could not afford to get his own place. Darren was living in the old car that his late grandfather gave him. When he was asked about the money he received from staff—we found out he used it for food and gas. Travis Academy adopted the philosophy of 360 degrees of service. We found him a place to live with relatives because Darren could not function at his best sleeping in his car every night and eating very little food. It was our responsibility to help.

Our vocational model was not only about academics and a job, it also included relationships. We wanted to show love to angry teenagers who were mad at the world, and could not remember the last time anyone said, "I love you." Often when a teacher would reach out to touch a student, they would jerk back. *Don't touch me*, were words we heard frequently because our teenagers associated a loving touch with abuse. We tried to incorporate positive reinforcement to students using words that brought life and spoke to their potential. Each teacher would share a constructive comment each day to students in what we called their *Home Base Room*.

When teenagers entered school, most faces were either sad or angry; it was hard to find any resemblance of a smile. We were seeking to find what may be called their love language or relationship language of our students. Concentrating on our ability to connect and create a relationship with them, we provided a loving and nurturing classroom environment with a hand shake in the morning or a warm smile or friendly greeting.

Sometimes We Just Need Kind Words

Viola was a student who cursed a lot. She would not let anybody near her and kept a frown all day. Viola never participated in classroom activities. If any teacher approached her desk they could only stay a few seconds before she told them to go away. In staff meetings, teachers expressed concerns about her self- imposed isolation. Whenever I walked down the hallway, I would say hello, asked how she was feeling, then whisper, "You know you are my girl." She would never respond keeping her head down as I passed by. I tried complimenting her, again nothing from Viola.

On Fridays, many classrooms set up games and activities. Ninety-nine percent of the students found interest in something— not Viola, she sat in the corner quiet and sad. One week, I was out of town for a conference and when I returned, it happened to be on Friday afternoon. The students were engaged in their activities, there was Viola again in the corner alone. When I walked into the room she rose to her feet, clapped her hands and smiled. Then she said with excitement "Dr. Travis is back, Dr. Travis is back!" Wow something did matter to her! We were all shocked, but very pleased. Finally, a breakthrough. The staff recognized that Viola did receive our compliments— made evident by her response. Teachers continued to say nice things to her. Little by little, Viola began to warm up and gave us permission to enter to her space. She improved her attitude and replaced her failing grades with B's and C's. Mission accomplished!

In our high school journey, we had to understand the multitude of needs from an emotional and academic standpoint. We wanted to produce a well- rounded student to function in society. The advancement of technology soon became an issue; every child wanted to be on the cutting edge of technology. Resources were being made available in the community, we could see that in our vocational model, we had students who did not exactly fit. Should we start another high school with a technology focus?

The Technological Shift

Bill and Melinda Gates Foundation gave technology based grants in Milwaukee to establish high schools with 300 students or less enrolled. We talked about the possibilities with our board and agreed to submit a proposal and application to receive funding. Staff felt that as we trained our students, we should offer a feeder high school to meet their technology needs.

Our school was selected to receive the grant from the Bill and Melinda Gates Foundation, and we accepted the challenge to start Travis Technology High School. It was developed to give opportunities to students in music, video tech and graphic arts.

Applying for the grant afforded us funding dollars to visit other schools in different cities around the country such as Portland, Boston, San Diego and Chicago, where we could observe operations to move ahead. As the curriculum plans were being developed, I began to ask God for a new school building. We looked for months and found nothing. Out of the blue a local construction company called to tell me about a building on Stevens Road that would be ideal for us. We notified our bankers at Legacy Bank and offered a plan to purchase the building. One major problem surfaced, it was not zoned for school use. A petition was made before the Board of Zoning Appeals (BOZA). I called my prayer warriors at the time, my Aunt Pearl Harps in Greenville, Mississippi and Pastor Brenda Fruster in Tampa, Florida. We felt like we were up a creek without a paddle, but we activated our faith. Aunt Pearl prayed daily, and Brenda came to Milwaukee three months prior to the zoning meeting to pray. We received word that the zoning board denied our request for an occupancy permit. *Denied Lord, what am I going to do?* A hearing date was scheduled before the board to reconsider. I was already disappointed about the denial and could not understand my need to attend. I believed in my spirit the Lord said for me go. So, I went. I walked in that meeting with our realtor Jenni Green, and we sat until our school was called. The board's chairman invited me to speak on behalf of Travis Technology High School. As I approached the bench, I asked God to please guide my thoughts and words. I stated my case to explain the need in Milwaukee to reach low income families, so they too can be on the cutting edge of technology. The chairman called for a vote. Two members approved, the other two members denied the occupancy permit. The chairman said, "It's a tie therefore I must break the tie. Go and start your technology school." His answer was yes! I humbly said to God, "You are awesome in all your ways."

With occupancy permit in hand, we opened the doors to Travis Technology High School to 155 students the first year. Students like David made it worthwhile, he had been dropped from another tech high school. He underperformed in large classroom settings and required a smaller class to prevent distractions. David talked excessively and we had to constantly redirect him from that behavior. Unfocused most times, he was off task more than on, yet he had potential. Our graphic design teacher Ms. Latasha Jackson accepted the challenge of molding David. He beautifully designed holiday cards for Christmas and New Year with words from his handwritten collection of poetry. David exceled in graphic design, spoke well and turned out to be a good orator winning second place in a speech writing contest. He was one of the first students who entered our *Graphic Design Program* and after graduation David went to Central State University in Ohio.

Another student Desmond was masterful in music, graphics and video. Desmond also won second place winner in the annual

Martin Luther King, Jr. Speech and Writing Contest. Coincidently, he placed during our anniversary of ten years. We had secured actor Danny Glover as our speaker, alas due to the East Coast winter storms, that extended partly to the Midwest here in Milwaukee, he was delayed in Africa. These unfortunate circumstances turned fortunate, Danny decided to invite a student and two chaperones to be his guests at the premiere of Dream Girls in New York City with all expenses paid by him. Desmond's achievement gained him our selection to attend the opening along with two of our dedicated teachers Mr. Martin and Mrs. Brinson. He met many Hollywood and New York stars, and people from all walks of life. Desmond told us that he stood in the buffet line with Cedric the Entertainer, and shared other memorable experiences. At graduation, Desmond confidently posed as he walked across the stage. Pleasantly, he had been accepted to several colleges and his only decision was to select one.

Flourishing Interns and Artists

In our following years, approximately 220 students were enrolled at Travis Tech High and we strived to keep it at that level. Well known artist and graphic designer, Paul Houzell from California conducted a *Summer Intern Seminar* at tech high, which was a privilege to students and staff. Students had the opportunity to display some of their design work at various banks in Milwaukee and Ridgestone Bank in Brookfield. When the summer internship ended, Tech High was honored to be the recipient of an original painting by Paul Houzell.

TOMS
(TIPS ON MOVING STUDENTS)

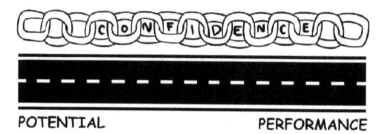

POTENTIAL   PERFORMANCE

- *Look beyond the problem or condition and see the need, meet that need*
- *Unique programs can be a drawing card*
- *You may be the only positive adult in the student's life*

CHAPTER FOURTEEN

AN ANGRY VIEW

Originally, I told myself that I was not going to mention Roger, I changed my mind. The reason is because it still pains me to this day, and drains my energy even to talk about this. Roger played a significant part that bears discussion, therefore he made the book. Roger was a client when I worked for the Milwaukee Wraparound Program. As I started Travis Academy, I looked for other financial avenues. Based on my counseling experience working with other agencies, I thought it would be an excellent way to supplement my income. Every dollar earned went to Travis Academy and needed to be spent on children or my staff with nothing left for me. Sadly, Roger was a very emotionally disturbed child. He was 11 years old with five different foster homes placements. The first time we met, he smiled some, especially when we went to McDonald's but it was obvious, he was troubled. We had conversations about his goals; one goal was Roger wanted to be close with his immediate family—and hoped one day to be placed with relatives.

We met once a week to discuss his thoughts and feelings. He attended regular public school; however, that did not last long. His school called to talk about his inability to control his mouth and physical assaultive behavior. In our sessions, I had interactive exercises with Roger. We would do what I called, *think-it-through* drills. For instance, What went wrong? What were my options? What should I do differently? After about ten meetings with school officials and teachers, I thought it best to switch Roger to Travis Academy. The aim was to work more intensely on his problems and keep a closer eye on him.

The second day at Travis Academy, Roger got into a fight. Another student said something that irritated him— then he left his seat and started punching this boy. His face and eyes swelled up in anger. I took him home to his foster mother and we sat down to discuss what happened. He had two days of time-out. When he returned to school, he rotated an hour working in the classroom and an hour near me; this arrangement worked well.

Roger's parents rejected him early; he really did not have a relationship with his family. He always longed to visit his mom and dad, but they had no desire to see him and left Roger in the foster care system. When his grandmother died, he found out and wanted to go the funeral. I contacted the foster care agency and informed them I would take him because we had established a close relationship and he trusted me. Once we arrived at the service, we observed his parents seated in the first row. Roger walked up to the casket, looked at his grandmother and stayed there for a while— then turned around and walked away. I said to Roger, "Is that your mom and dad sitting there?" He said, "Yes." I could not believe it. Those people watched this child go up to the casket, look at his deceased grandmother and never opened their mouths. We sat about midway in the church. Well, I could not take it anymore! I went up to the parents and said, "Hello, I am Roger's therapist, did you see him?" The mom replied, "Yes, yes, yes," I continued, "Well, it is my understanding that you have not seen this child in almost four years." With this look of guilt on her face, "Yeah, that's right, but I knew it was Roger when he came up." This entire situation upset me, no wonder he had trouble in foster care and school. "Ma'am, your son would like a bit more than a stare from you, next to a casket." There was silence. I continued, "Could you say hello to him, put your arms around him and give him a hug?" Reluctantly she said, "Well yeah, well yeah," Then I proceeded to get Roger so that he could speak to his mom. She managed to give him an unwelcomed hug. His dad was sitting next to her and said, "Hey Roger, you're getting fatter and you're getting taller, aren't you?" Those few words made him smile, he was happy to be talking to his parents who otherwise would have remain silent had I not said anything.

Back to the Drawing Board

We worked closely with Roger during seventh grade and his change was gradual. Like other students he was placed in our behavior modification system. It was a good system that was working for him. Roger was making progress, albeit slow but nevertheless progress! Then a relapse occurred, his foster mother called to inform me Roger fought one of his foster brothers. He went ballistic and broke the other child's foot with a can. Unable to calm Roger, his foster mother called police and the authorities took him to Children's Detention Center.

The next week, I went to see Roger, he understood what he did wrong. There were not any more options left for placement with foster homes. The social service agency had to place him in a group home for six months, which he did not like, but it was without incident, at least we thought. Roger was at it again. The group home worker called to inform us Roger was ignoring the rules. *Oh, my Lord*, I thought. *Is this child going to make it or not?* I went over to try and deescalate the situation. There he was cursing and acting like he had no self-control. Then he caught a glimpse of me, stopped and said, "Why are you wearing that color lipstick? It doesn't look good on you! You need to take it off!" I paused to collect my thoughts, "Wait a minute Roger, hold it! You are completely out of control, but have enough sense to stop and tell me about my lipstick?" That exchange told me he had some of his faculties. At my insistence he was sent to his room and not allowed to come out. We revisited his lessons on self-control to reestablish boundaries. Eventually, he returned to Travis Academy to complete his middle school studies with high school on the horizon.

Jailbirds Cannot Fly

Roger did not have a loving relationship with his parents, but the agency granted him home visits. Need I say more, it was a complete disaster! He went over to see them, and a brawl broke out with his mom. He had a knife, mom had a knife they were ready to cut each other. This melee caused Roger to be removed from the group home into detention and later to Kettle Moraine Correctional Institution in Wisconsin. While he was there, I went to visit him like I would do for many other boys who were former or current incarcerated students.

Once time came for his release I decided we were not going to allow him to ride the bus with other prisoners to be reintroduced to the community. My friend Ruby Wiley and I drove to Kettle Moraine to pick him up. On the ride back, we agreed Roger would continue his studies at Travis Academy and he was registered for high school. After all we had been through, he no longer called me Ms. Travis, he called me "Mom."

Time to Graduate, Time to Grow

Roger was oldest boy in the senior class. We gave him the added responsibility to work in building maintenance to boost his character. He was very helpful and proud of what he was doing! Graduation day arrived, Roger had to make some adult decisions about his life. He never had parental love and Travis Academy did our best to help him. Roger missed the formative years without the affection of a mother. Maybe, that was why he involved himself with an older woman, which concerned me. That also became a problem with several of our boys because some women were ten or more years older than them.

Roger working for us came with its own set of problems. Following directions was not his strong suit—he refused to accept orders from his supervisor. He ran to my office hoping I would side with him. To the contrary I said, "You have to follow the instructions of your supervisor." Well, after I refused to intervene on his behalf, he got angry. My heart ached because I thought we had come a long way with his anger. Then, Roger declared to the staff that he would destroy the place - he even would kill! That outburst made staff fearful and they wanted to call the police. Hard decisions had to be made, I did not want this [grown]child to go back to prison. I wanted to still give him an opportunity, I told staff not to call the police. Rather, usher him out of the school and let think the police were called. Tell Roger we do not want to see anymore again.

The next week Roger called. I sternly said," I do not want to talk to you. You threatened the safety of people in our building. Several staff members were afraid that you might harm them." He paused for a moment with a denial, "I didn't really say that" Then added, "I didn't really mean it, you know I didn't mean it," My decision was firm Roger could not come back. I told him, "There are people around this country who have made the same threat and carried them out! Why would we think any different? We do not know what you are thinking." I believed wholeheartedly that he would not harm anyone nonetheless, my [feelings] were not a 100% guarantee!

The End Draws Near

Weeks passed, Roger called to apologize. I am sorry, it was not enough time to repair the damage. The wound was too deep and hurtful, my devotion to Roger was sincere and real. And I have no regrets about helping him. So, it could be asked, *Is this unconditional love in place or did it go out of the window?* No, it did not, as much as you want to love someone with every corner of your heart, I have learned that you cannot always love up close.

This portion of my journey revealed my responsibility to our children was never an easy undertaking. Sometimes, we must be released from the ones we love and who hurt us most. A known psychologist once said that people who have the inability to disconnect from a person (like Roger) simply means that these people possess love in their heart to connect with others. Well, I am guilty as charged by association of my heart.

TOMS
(TIPS ON MOVING STUDENTS)

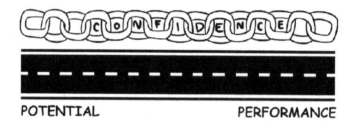

POTENTIAL   PERFORMANCE

- *Keep a watch on emotions, they can trigger out of control*
- *Learn to forgive, it is a health medicine*
- *Willingness to allow your passion to continue when tested is a virtue*

CHAPTER FIFTEEN

ONE ACCORD

Every Tuesday after 3:45 PM dismissal, we held staff meetings. Usually the principal or assistant principal conducted these sessions to review progress. The agenda consisted of questions, concerns, announcements and plans. This time was often used to decompress from the problems we faced daily. Most times it gave us the opportunity to determine what worked and what needed to change. We were operating three schools with a total of 70 staff members, and we tried to prioritize discussions with teachers and presenters who gave their assessments for the week.

I wanted to create an environment for staff to be refreshed and relaxed, I did not want our first meeting in September to become mundane, so the staff would show their creativity with a whimsical introduction. Staff meetings were a high energy time and I enjoyed encouraging and communicating with my staff. These meetings unified us, and relationships were built. Every year we used a different theme to make sure we served the children. One year we used the idea from Dr. Robert Pavlik, through symbolism of the traffic signal. The same principle of stop and go applied to our methods for effective operation. Green light meant that things were working well, and those practices should be continued. Yellow light meant cautionary measures should be taken and reevaluation was needed. Red light meant we needed to stop completely and go back to the drawing board. This help me to fully reexamine the mission of Travis Academy. We were a team who had to push students at risk of failing because they had no support, proper formative instruction or economic freedom. Inspiring them was vital to the success of the students. I shared the story of the father and son cruising from New York to Europe at sea. How they could see way out unto the horizon. It was midnight in New York and due to the eight -hour time difference, it meant sunrise was on another shore. They witnessed darkness behind them and sunlight in front. They stood in awe of God's handiwork. However, the little boy could not see; then his father placed him shoulder high to see the sunlight. After a couple of minutes of gazing out until yonder, the father asked the son if he could see. The son replied, "Yes I can see farther than my eyes can go." I used this tale to impress upon staff members that they needed to see farther than their eyes could go. Children came to school with all sorts of physical and emotional pain. And sometimes they may not respond —the way you wanted them to respond. It is good to step back and not behold the child in that moment, but see beyond. In other words, see the possibilities in children and in each other. Our goal was to create an excellent curriculum that spoke to their needs and have a leadership team designed to motivate and develop the best. As the founder of the school, I considered myself the key motivator.

Acts of Kindness

I loved to surprise the staff with acts of kindness. We got paid every other Friday and many times on the non-pay day Friday, I would give a small gift of appreciation to staff. A thank you note, drinks or donut or pens are simple ways to let the staff know how valuable they are to the school. During the first month, my staff received a Payday Candy bar and a note inscribed *You deserve a PAY DAY because your hard work is paying off. ENJOY!* Other times it was a 100 GRAND bar. *You are worth a 100 grand for all you do for student.* At staff meetings, another fun way was with a cold caffeinated drink with this note, *Have a Coke and a Smile.* Teachers and staff are often exhausted in the afternoon, this serves as a pick-me-up for *on the way* home. There are millions of ways to show how much you care when an effort is made to find them.

Act of kindness can be explored in many ways. The main thing is to recognize that teachers and staff members have problems and issues like the rest of the world. We need to show love. If you have a great staff, you can make it greater through sincere appreciation.

Community Leaders Honored

An African Proverb says, *it takes a whole village to raise a child.* I have always believed the *village* should be included in school activities. Businesses were sought out to employ our students, we asked them for incentives to give out at awards ceremonies and events throughout the year. We discovered this inspired our students and they loved to receive paper certificates with *Job Well Done,* on it, even more they loved the McDonald's meal coupons which meant dinner for many students. Communities leaders and businesses owners were invited to share in our career day programs. Students could interact and ask questions to police officers, firefighters, social workers, nurses and local judges to name a few. It brought delight to our students to see pillars of the community encourage and share lunch with them. Soon, we began to ask students to invite parents, grandparents, and other relatives who were important in their lives to lunch. Also, we decided to create a *Community Hero* theme and hold an annual luncheon for community leaders every February to honor seven individuals, because the number seven represents completion. With the criteria set, students nominated people who made a difference in their community like the neighbor who babysat free of charge, the man who saved the cat, the woman who reported illegal drug traffic or the corner store owner who helped people. Of course, a special lunch was prepared, and the children entertained our honorees and guest with songs, poems and danced as part of the Performing Arts.

The Guiding Light

The school's administrator should embrace the role of instructional leader to staff and students. This person sets the tone for the school's success or failure. It is important to bring staff together and equally important to offer guidance. Micromanaging suffocates the staff and produces resentment, and no one benefits. The entire staff carries a tremendous load and they are human too. They have ideas, opinions and constructive criticism and sometimes just plain criticism. Moreover, they have voices that need to be heard, they are ones in the classroom dealing with students. Administrators must consider what is best for students and staff without in-house politics or better yet outside politics involved. Mainly, the focus should be on academics, social skills, and behavior. I tried to encourage my administrators to exhibit an atmosphere of high expectations and it did not matter if the students came to us with all sorts of negative behavior that was their starting point.

We have the responsibility to take them further and treat them with dignity and respect. Some children will come with low academics and social skills, but high expectations still should be in place, because some parents do not have any —that is part of the problem —wisdom must be used. It should be crystal clear that we believe in them and will love and nourish them. A warm school climate signifies help and devotion to its students. Negative attitudes or discouragement have no place in education. I remember we had a student arrived late to school and I observed a security employee talking to him. "Where is your note to return to school?" he asked the young man. And the student said, "I don't have one" and the security officer interrupted before he finished his sentence, "You know you need one. You haven't been to school in seven days. I suggest you get a note before you try to come back here." It was time to intervene. Not to undermine the security's authority I asked, "What were you were trying to say young man? I did not hear the rest of your sentence." Notice, I did not try to embarrass the security officer by telling him, "You should not be so mean and let him finish his statement." Instead, I stepped up to model another approach to the situation. The young man told me that his mother was in jail. He was staying with his granddad who brought him to school. "Come on in", I said as I looked at the security guard. "Let's see if we can get granddad on the phone and see how we can help you." Although the security was following procedure you cannot make students, especially high- risk students feel rejected or frightened.

Later, I explained to the security officer that I was modeling an alternative way of handling the situation. Sometimes it is not just stick to the hard and fast rule, you must trust your heart, I challenged him to trust that. Leadership must be the guiding force to provide a safe and orderly environment for all its students I strongly believe that. There is a scripture in Habakkuk 2:2 that says in part, *Write the vision on the tablet and make it plain,* and the guiding light for all employees is understanding the vision. Teachers and staff can create a structured environment to promote order and disciplined. Classroom rules need to be clearly explained and enforced by all teachers and staff. Behaviors can change, if students understand what is required of them. I believe that all students want to learn. I cannot stress the importance of meeting student's needs and being in sync to their directions and goals. Setting up the right program can be trial and error, it may sound like a workable program, yet after implementation it does not work. You cannot simply force it, I have seen teachers try to push an ineffective curriculum on students. Administrators must watch for the warning signs and know when to replace it. The light will shine brighter if the administrators and staff are on one accord. In addition to the curriculum, the discipline matters, safety issues, parent concerns, and food service problems—there were often concerns in the personal lives of staff members. We were a family and we tried to exhibit a family atmosphere, one of care and concern. My duty was to be the champion for teachers and support them in their classroom activities and out of the classroom. Just like students, the staff will also have different personalities and teaching styles. Even inside of every rule, method or procedure, there still must be flexibility when dealing with teachers. Some freedoms should be allowed if it does not interfere with the core vision. Once again, they work in the classroom and they can determine students need the best. Remember, leadership and guidance will ensure proper balance.

The Scales Tipped

Early one morning I walked into a teacher's classroom and saw ten disciplinary slips filled out, complete with date and teacher's signature. Naturally, I was curious. "What makes you think that you will have ten students in need of administrator's intervention today," I asked. While she was thinking of an answer, I had to ask why she did not have ten good job slips filled out on her desk too. We talked for several weeks as I demonstrated ways to improve the atmosphere in the classroom to produce more positive than negative results. At -risk students particularly are not always less intelligent, quite the contrary. Sadly, they have been subjected to poor living conditions, abuse, rejection, and truancy problems caused by parents not sending them to school. These are real issues they have no control over, educators must learn how to identify these issues. We cannot see them as failures, menaces to society or worthless human beings who do not deserve a chance at life, if we buy into these cultural stereotypes, then they are just children without hope. Sure, when educators are overworked and underpaid, it is difficult to always be understanding. However, the irony is that federal, state and local governments that vote on massive reductions in education funding was once served by the very [public] system that produced the politicians in favor of the cuts.

Everyone from top down needs to be supported. My desire was to make sure our staff could handle the complexities of teaching children who were not physically orphaned but mentally orphaned get the education they needed to learn how to dream or dream bigger than their circumstances. Sometimes teachers just could not see our school's vision which was fine and they were free to search for other career alternatives.

TOMS
(TIPS ON MOVING STUDENTS)

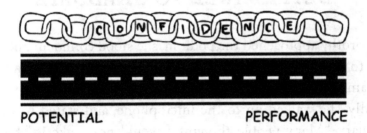

POTENTIAL   PERFORMANCE

- *Serve the staff with gladness, working with challenging learners can be stressful*
- *Push staff to greatness and see possibilities in all*
- *Eliminate that which does not work*

CHAPTER SIXTEEN

DETERMINED TO GRADUATE

Dorothy approached the podium, she stood confident and ready to deliver the graduation speech. Coincidentally, we have the same name, which I thought was unusual for her young age. Proudly, she walked up to the microphone, and stated to the full sanctuary, "Many people thought I would not make it." Seconds into the speech tears rolled down her face. "I lost my mother, so I had to find a way to survive. Some thought that was end for me, I kept going then I lost my baby." Suddenly, she broke almost falling to her knees; Morgyn Gathering, Student Coordinator, rushed to her side, after getting composed the speech continued, "I got to get it out. I want the world to know I made it! You do the same. Don't be ashamed of your past. Today we can tell the world we are somebody." You could hear a pin dropped until she invited the entire graduation class to say, "We made it!" The sound of thundering voices erupted with joy, what a momentous occasion it was!

In 2003, our first high school graduation was held from Travis Academy Vocational High School Program. Graduations were always moving, it captured children who struggled daily battling life crisis to walk across the stage and receive their diploma. The large crowd of roughly 700 or 800 parents, relatives and friends cheered them on. Many students started out with us as six graders. This celebration meant families could experience their children's achievement with joy. Sadly, some students did not have parents who cared enough to attend. I remember one student name Kyle was upset that no one from his family came to see him graduate. He stood by the side of a church pew, his eyes filled with tears. I tried to console him, "It's okay. You made it and you had great determination deep down on the inside of you". Many times, he wanted to quit because Kyle thought he could not solve math problems or write a good enough research paper. I reminded him that our teachers pulled him through every [class] phrase. "Don't worry about who is not here" I said, "Be happy for yourself, your classmates are happy for you. Kyle, your teachers are happy for you, in fact I am very happy for you." And then I whispered, "You are not alone, other students are here without family too." I wanted to help in a small way to relieve their sadness and treated the entire group to graduation dinner.

Travis Academy specialized in giving students a renewed life. We were like surrogate parents to students who were raising themselves. There were students who lived in their own apartments in junior year. They were left to survive in an adult world —still these children needed direction because independent students were hard to reach, and we pushed them to graduate.

These Shoes Were Made for Walking

I want to speak about Drew, he spent six years trying to get through high school. His family life was unstable, they fought frequently and moved every other month. I can recall one situation when his mother and grandmother fought over the same man. His grandmother stabbed his mother in a domestic dispute. The police got involved, both were hospitalized, then landed in jail for the weekend. The electricity in the home had been disconnected and Drew's younger siblings stayed wherever they could. This poor student told us for three nights he slept at the park and bus station until their release. Through every obstacle he faced, we worked with him until he graduated.

In his senior year, Drew entered the annual Martin Luther King, Jr. Writing and Speech Contest. Students would research the theme provided to us by *We Energies* and the Milwaukee Public Schools' committee. According to grade level, there were different categories and each classroom would hold individual contests. The winners from each classroom would pair up with another student in their category. Everything this young man endured, he still wrote a dynamic speech. For over a month, I rehearsed with him daily until he memorized every word. Sometimes he was absent due to family drama and tensions. The weekend before the speech contest I asked him to wear something nice. We talked about his wardrobe and what he needed to do to prepare for Monday's afternoon speech.

He showed up on Monday with the same clothes worn on Friday. The look on his emotionally wrecked face gave away that something went terribly wrong. A fight occurred between him and his sister on the previous Friday and their mother made Drew leave. Again, he was left to wander the streets with no place to go. Now what? We had an emergency here. Drew needed to take a shower and get some clothes. Stories like this were common. Still my heart ached for students when I heard their horrifying story. Quickly, I had to get a plan, Drew was speaking in three hours. I called my husband Felton for help and asked could he take Drew clothes shopping at Walmart. My office was in an old Catholic Rectory with three apartments where the priests once lived. Two apartments had full bathrooms, Drew used one and showered there. Within minutes my husband picked him up, which lifted a heavy weight off us. Right in the nick of time they returned for Drew's debut. Minutes later he appeared cleaned and neatly dressed looking sharp. We went over his speech for the final time, then I prayed over him. Drew was grateful and as my husband was leaving he said, "Thank you Mr. Moore."

He did not place at the contest, but received an honorable mention, I was happy Drew achieved that success. It is not always about being first place, sometimes it is more about commitment, passion, focus and not giving up. You win that way, it is how students learn to be competitive, not with others, but with themselves— which is a more valuable lesson. Drew presented an excellent speech and in my eyes, he was a winner. The weeks remaining, he completed his graduation requirements. A delightful moment happened when he walked across the stage, Drew finished what he started. All he needed was people to care about his future.

Fifty Percent is Not Enough

Dean was another senior who attended school about half of the time. Polite and determined described his personality. He did not like to miss assignments, when he did he would ask for make-up work and returned every lesson completed. Constantly, our team would talk to him about his overall attendance. He had a courteous personality and he promised to do better. It was brought to the school administrator's attention that Dean was living in his car. Mrs. Brinson asked teacher Mr. Martin to investigate. We found this to be true and our team set out to find a [temporary] place for him and we successfully located a men's shelter that provided food and shower facilities. Despite his living arrangements and attendance issues he was determined to graduate. Dean told us nothing could stop him. Nothing did. Not only did he graduate, but he found a job making a decent wage. His life was changed.

The Big Surprise

Let me introduce Tina, she was an 18 -year old honor roll student who made coming to school her priority! Tina's stellar grades qualified her for placement at Subway by our work experience specialist, along with other classmates from tech high. As long as students had passing grades, they were eligible to be placed for employment. Tina earned her way to shift manager, worked 40 hours a week, attended school every day and impressively she was never tardy. Focused on her studies, often she asked, "How am I doing?" We let her know she was doing well and encouraged her to continue. This was huge for Tina, she was the youngest of ten children. None of her siblings including her mother ever received a high school diploma. So you see this was something special for the family. The day she walked across the stage her entire family came to cheer her on. Surprisingly, three weeks after graduation Tina delivered a baby boy. No one knew! There was no denying, she was the hardest working student in the graduating class. Pure determination!

A Storm Without Rain

Graduation sometimes was marked with students who weathered many life storms. I talked about Michael in an earlier chapter, he started when Travis Academy first opened; his story is slightly different from the others. Upset that his mother, his aunt nor his uncle came to the ceremony, his only support system was his pregnant girlfriend who had graduated days earlier. Michael attended church, his strong sense of faith made him want to do the right thing and marry his girlfriend. Later that June, Michael and his girlfriend got married. Most times, students would plan for college, not for a wedding. But at least they headed in the right direction. To my surprise, Michael joined the Army and went to New Jersey for basic training. After training he was deplored overseas to Iraq. I remember one summer's night in August while attending the African World festival, I received a call from Michael before he left for Iraq. He said, "Just in case I don't make it back, I want you to know that I would not be the man that I am without the help of Travis Academy." I prayed for his safety and thanked God for our many graduations because students could fulfill dreams, utilize skills, and perform duties that served this country and their neighborhood.

TOMS
(TIPS ON MOVING STUDENTS)

POTENTIAL   **PERFORMANCE**

- *Graduation turns potential to performance allowing students to feel success*
- *Sacrifice to bring joy, it's worthwhile*
- *Promote healthy relationship*

CHAPTER SEVENTEEN

THE GOD MOTHER

In search for a better life, this single mother left Chicago and made her way to Milwaukee. Tired, hungry and being afraid was enough motivation to change her unfavorable circumstances. She lived in a shelter for three months with her eight children, while she looked for a job. In the meantime, she needed to enroll her children in school. A recruiter for Travis Academy went to the shelter to locate truant students, six of her eight children were eligible to attend after missing school for several weeks. The children grades ranged from second to tenth grades. The mother was relieved and in her words, *were answered prayers.*

After procuring an office job for a trucking company— she moved out from the shelter into a small apartment of their own. The place was not quite big enough for her family, but she had no complaints, this mother learned how to make things work. I will never forget her name Shekeela Wingard because said she instantly, *felt the connection* with her family and Travis Academy, she said, "It's never pleasant to admit that you don't have clothes or school supplies for your children, but with the teachers at Travis Academy, I didn't feel embarrassed, I really felt genuine concern."

This young mother confessed with eight children, she did not know how to make it sometimes.

On the very first day, when school started her children did not have uniforms nor clean clothes. Immediate action was required! We had to do something, these children needed to be in school. The staff rallied together went shopping to purchase clothing and essentials for the family. The smile on that mother's face was priceless. One of her younger boys Eric would see me in the hallways and say, "Hi momma!" I did not want to discourage him, but I said with a gentle tone, "It is Dr. Travis and how are you doing today?" At morning meditation, he came over to me and finally said, "Hi Dr. Travis!" As I walked away, it was, "Bye momma." Noted psychologists say that it is not uncommon for children to identify another figure as a parent when that person nurtures and cares like one. Moreover, they say oftentimes the female figure are referred to as mother or godmother.

The oldest child Jerrell was a sophomore when he came to the Academy. He made it through, his whole family was in full support when he graduated. Ms. Wingard expressed how happy she was for her son to be the first to graduate from high school. "I never graduated, now we have a high school graduate." The second son Jaden experienced more behavioral problems than Jerrell. In fact, he was expelled from Travis Academy. During that time, he was sent back to Chicago to live with his dad to finish the school year. That arrangement did not work out Jaden's father never placed him in school. Jaden returned to Milwaukee and we had a long re-instatement conference. Since, his period of expulsion was **over** Jaden was welcomed back. Ms. Wingard had six boys and two girls. One of her daughters was quite ambitious. Nia suffered from a serious medical condition, but that never deterred her. She completed the eighth grade with honors and transitioned into our tech high. She would affectionately say, "You are our godmother." These were touching words that made me feel appreciated and I will never apologize for helping children.

This mother went through a crisis of poor health, she had about six major surgeries with two more scheduled. She applied to receive benefits from Social Security and they denied her over and over. Limited resources caused mounting bills and the rent needed to be paid.

Ms. Wingard called me panicked and in tears. I could hear the children's voices in the background, when she said, "Dr. Travis I hate to call you but we're in real trouble. The sheriff's here to evict us and our things are on the lawn. We don't really have a place to go. I'm going to try and see if I can take my family over to my sister's and a lady at church will store our things." She asked the bailiff to talk to the landlord, but too much money was owed. Ms. Wingard asked if I could loan her $600. I made the decision to give her the money without any expectation repayment, this family was in need. I rushed to my bank's Automated Teller Machine (ATM), retrieved the money, then headed over to her house. Personally, I have never witnessed anything like this before— her appliances, furniture and clothes were sprawled all over the lawn. Two of the boys noticed me and ran to the car shouting, "Dr. Travis is here, Dr. Travis is here! One said, "Yes, our momma is here." They had the biggest smiles on their faces. I handed their mother the money and as I drove away, one said "Thank you momma, I mean Dr. Travis." At that point, I did not mind being called momma or godmother.

Concerned about this family, I checked back with Ms. Wingard who was a resilient woman who knew how to bounce back, refusing to be depressed or unhappy. Her middle son Jacob experienced behavioral problems and had to repeat the eighth grade. I thought she would be upset, only to the contrary, she felt Jacob did not work hard and needed another year to grow up. In fact, she became every helpful around the school. We hosted a back to school barbeque, and her contribution was homemade soap for all the parents. Also, her soap was sold locally at the flea market and proceeds were donated for our fundraiser. She was actively involved and elected as vice-president of our Parent Teacher Organization (PTO).

Like any family, some of her children were doing well and some struggled. Ms. Wingard continued to have financial difficulties. Her daughter Nia decided to go and live with her dad in Arkansas— that did not work out. She returned to Milwaukee and decided to go to a community school. The next summer she entered the *Ms. Juneteenth Pageant* and won the crown! It seemed like once I connect with a family, it is forever. I believe the *godmother* role keeps me in the forever status.

Things Need to Compute

Nia was an ambitious young lady, after graduation she received a scholarship to college. The first day on campus was met with anxiety— Nia called me hysterical. At orientation her instructor told the class they must have a [laptop] computer for course assignments. Nia's dad promised to send her one, but failed to come through. Her family could not afford to furnish a computer for her. Nia made it to college, it was not the time for her to turn back and we were not going to let her. She asked, "Dr. Travis do you have a laptop?" In about a week, I delivered a laptop to her. An educator does more than teach reading and math; we unwrap their gifts, and unleash their talents. Someone must stand with students in times of trouble to pick up the slack as godmothers or godfathers.

Still Carrying the Wand

Holy boldness was required to accomplish the necessary things, when working with an at-risk student population. Truancy was a major problem. I have seen this too much, it usually leads good or bad students to failure. Brian was 16 years old, a good kid with extremely poor attendance. He was happy go lucky, a jokester and smiled all the time. Brian was left to care for himself, his mother frequently stayed at her boyfriend's place. He was not attending school and we called to inquire about the reason. We heard one excuse after the other, Brian was repeating ninth grade and needed five credits to move from freshman to sophomore. Every school he transferred from— there was not enough credit earned to get promoted. Brian's mother decided to move into her cousin's household. This type of instability often leads to many students' absence from school and not passing to the proper grade. Thankfully, her cousin referred Brian to Travis Academy because she had four boys in our school. We understood this problem when Brian enrolled that year. He started off good during September and October averaging about 70% attendance, not the greatest. I still made it my business to compliment Brian every day that he came. The first week in November no one from that household was in school. We threatened to call the authorities because the law stated that parents may be fined or arrested for non-compliance of mandatory attendance rules. We had already mailed out truancy letters to the home and no parent or guardian responded. It was confirmed by the children again, Brian's mother basically lived at her boyfriend's house.

The first quarter ended. I noticed Brian had fallen into that same pattern of poor attendance and failing grades. One of our security personnel took Brian under his wings because he saw possibilities in him. According to him, the move Brian's mother made with her cousin was not the best living arrangement and homelessness was a step away. This security member mentioned that when Brian attended school, he would do his work. Further, he stated that his cousins seem real hardcore. All of them had been incarcerated at least twice. Information was passed onto me these cousins may have been attending school to expand their drug reach. I probed more about this. The security member stated these boys constantly watched him, which is a known indicator of dealing drugs or some other illegal activity. I asked him, "Was anything ever found?" He informed me, they can hide drugs outside or wherever, but never found anything on them. Troubled by Brian's home environment I spoke with his homeroom teacher to see if he could earn credits if he showed up and put forth an effort.

The thing that bothered me was Brian made unkept promises about coming to school, I would rarely see him. Brian was in-charge of himself, since his mother was barely around.

My spirit was disturbed, and I asked the Lord what to do. I ended up calling Brian's house that afternoon. He answered the phone, as usual he was gracious and said he would be at school the following day, then I advised him tell your cousins to get to school also. Before we hung up, I said to him, "Brian I am going to hold you to your word, I want to see you in school tomorrow." The next day I looked for Brian. Attendance was taken by 9:00 AM and guess who was on the absentee list? I did my morning walk through the speaking to students, staff and parents, for some reason I could not take my mind off Brian. I thought maybe he might show up before noon. It was not long before my watch displayed 11:45 AM. Something rose inside of me, I could feel that holy boldness again. Moments later, I got in my car and drove to Brian and his cousin's house. I sat in front for two minutes preparing my game plan.

Not a Friendly Home Visit

As I marched up the broken wooden steps, I asked the Holy Spirit for strength. I figured they are probably still in the bed. I stood there for a couple of seconds, then I banged on the door with every inch of strength in my wrist. I banged until someone answered; it was Brian's voice. "It is me Dr. Travis, open up this door." He opened the door, and I could see boys and girls lying all over the place. I walked through the door like a mad woman. "It is noon," I shouted, "What are you all still doing in bed? The world is not going to wait on you all day, you need to be in school." I kept my voice in a shouting tone. "I am not going to tolerate you laying here and you are supposed to be in our school. Did anyone teach you right from wrong?" I looked at the girls and asked, "What are these girls doing here?" One boy shouted, "This is my girlfriend." Walking from the living room to the kitchen I said, "But she is not your wife, you need to get up and go to school." Afterwards, Brian told me their clothes were washing. "Well you better get down there and get them out. This is a shame. You are not doing anything with your life and it will not happen while you are in my school. I want you to get up and get dressed and get to the school by 2:00 PM today. If I do not see you at school by the deadline, I will call every Social Service office in the city and you better believe I know a few." I walked out the house slamming the door behind me. I got in the car, took a deep breath and said out loud, "The things you do for the sake of the children Dorothy."

I waited for Brian and his cousins to show up. At nearly 2:00 PM, they finally arrived. I had already complied assignments from teachers for him to work on. Before leaving school, I told him to come to my office. Brian did not leave until early evening. What I saw was a child in need of help. When he finished, we went to McDonald's for dinner. I told him that every day he came to school, I would make sure he ate dinner. Brian came to school most days for the remainder of the year. I contacted a local agency to assist him; he finally passed to the tenth grade. We managed to enroll him into a mentoring program to help him succeed. One day his mentor called to give us a progress report and asked to speak to Brian's godmother, Dr. Travis. Vividly I remember picking up the phone and saying, "Yes, she is speaking." There had to be at least a couple hundred students who would call me something related to the word "Mother."

TOMS
(TIPS ON MOVING STUDENTS)

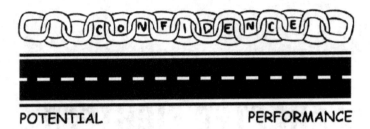

POTENTIAL   PERFORMANCE

- *Give yourself permission to be bold*
- *Understand what you are willing to do personally for students*
- *Loving others is a must and a positive name can connect to those in need*

CHAPTER EIGHTEEN

360 DEGREES OF SERVICE

One morning on my way to visit a third- grade classroom I observed our second graders on bathroom break. I heard one little boy shouting, "I told you [expletive] that I was going to [expletive] you up, I'm not playing with you [expletive]. I will blow your head off." Fill in the blanks, this came from a 7 year-old. Next thing I know his fist was balled tight, shoulders raised and his face had an expression that would scare a bear. I walked closer to him only to hear, "Touch me one more time[expletive]! Figuring out what to say was a struggle, I needed to connect with him, but his anger overshadowed my thoughts. "Let's speak kind words to each other, I am not hearing kind words." then paused to ask. "What is wrong?" He never looked at me— he kept looking at the other student who apparently touched him. He flinched at the boy "Just do it again [expletive]!" He went too far. "Enough I will not tolerate that language." In the vicinity was his teacher, she walked over whispering, "I will get him. Corey is having a very bad day." He exhibits this kind of behavior a lot, she explained. *What is the problem?* I thought. To bring balance for his actions, he received consequences for his negative language.

The next day I met with the teacher. She pointed out there was abuse in the home that made Corey angry. He was unable to read or write, I told her to quickly get him signed up for the Title 1 program. Title 1 is a government sponsored funding designed to help for low income students two years or more behind in reading or math. I decided to pay his mother a visit to determine the severity of the abuse. Surprisingly, the house was neat, although it smelled of marijuana. His mother tried to cover up her embarrassment by claiming while she was asleep her boyfriend had been smoking. I was not interested in that, my only interest concerned her son. This mother instantly labeled Corey as a behavior problem. "I'm going to just have to plan for Social Security," she said. Instead of getting to the root of the problem, she planned his future without giving Corey a chance. I had to respond, "Oh no, do not be so quick to label him, you must work with him." Getting more in depth, I suggested that his positive skills be used and developed. I also told her to commend him when he does something good. We discussed a reward system to build self- esteem to produce proper behavior.

I impressed upon her the importance of monitoring the filthy language used around him that Corey imitated in school. It was not long before she started to confess about her boyfriend's violent history and Corey's fear. She mentioned the difficulty of finding employment. We discussed job listings for her to explore. She continued to talk more about her boyfriend, from what I gathered, it seemed like she knew the answer. This mother just needed the strength to leave and make it safe for them. While there I discovered this family had no food in the house, with a little time left before returning to school, I took her grocery shopping.

At week's end, I dropped by Corey's classroom. I walked over to him and complimented his pretty eyes, eventually he looked up, that made me smile. I personally observed his progress. It was a slow gain, but still he progressed. I made it to Corey's class twice a week when I noticed his uniform shirt and pants were untidy. I sought out other people to become involved with Corey.

One of our cafeteria employees, Ms. Doris May told Corey that he looked like her grandson. Out of pure kindness, she purchased a new uniform for him. This generous act changed his disposition, "Ms. May is my friend," he said. Soon, we allowed him to empty cafeteria trays to earn a dollar.

Several months later, I picked up a lunch from the cafeteria and was on my way back to my office. Corey followed me as I exited the cafeteria, he did not say much. I let him know he was turning into a great learner and asked, "How things were going?" Nonchalantly he said, "It's okay. Are we going to get the Christmas gifts this year?" Softly I replied, "Yes, every student will receive a Christmas gift." With those precious eyes looking up at me, he thought for a moment, "May I have a hug?" I wrapped my arms around this little boy who was once so angry. This moment really brought me deep emotion— it was hard to keep it together and hold back the tears in my eyes but somehow, I managed. What a [great]blessing to see students improve their behavior. I loved it!

Lifelong Connections

We were approaching our 15th anniversary. The tuxedo shop manager called to say that most of the young men had been fitted for tuxes except for one, Samuel. "He needs to hurry in, so I can get him ready for the anniversary gala." he said. There was a lot of excitement in the air, we could hardly stand it. Most of it was coming from me; I was thanking God for His many wonderful blessings and placing His hand graciously upon our ministry. When I started Travis Academy, I specifically asked God for 15 years. He granted my request making this anniversary a beautiful occasion. International guests were present along with guests from all over the city and country. Everyone was dressed up, enjoyed themselves and looked great that evening. It was a celebratory event of thanksgiving to the Lord for favor, grace and mercy.

Before the anniversary, I could not help thinking about the problem we had locating Samuel. Our first three students, student Durrell,

Fred and Michael were participating along with several other students from various years who graduated from Travis Academy. But Samuel was still missing! I searched through my phone to find Samuel's number to call him. "Samuel, where are you?" I asked. "Hey Mama D (that is what he called me), my car broke down" That was not good. "Did you call someone?" He had called his uncle to come and start his car, then headed to the tuxedo shop. "Well, you better hurry, the tuxedo man said that you are running out of time." He made it to the shop in time and these former students made a great impression marching in ceremonial fashion at the anniversary celebration.

Samuel and I had history together. He was one of those young men I worried about in the early days. Thank God for bringing him through! Samuel and his two brothers were chronic truants from school. During our recruitment period, we found this family—I invited the mother to put her children in Travis Academy. Samuel was youngest of three boys. The difficulties we faced struggling to get them to school day-by-day challenged us. Unexpectedly, we received some heart-breaking news. One of the boys came to school and announced their mom just passed away. *Oh no my God! What are these boys going to do?* had me wondering. I went to their home to see how to help. I was really concerned about the boys, most of all, Samuel! He was the son who clung to his mother. Once funeral arrangements were complete I attended the services. The family seemed disconnected to the three boys at the funeral. They walked around talking to each other— ignoring the boys who sat alone in the back of the church. "Why you are all sitting in the back of the church?", I asked! I did not even wait for a response, "Come on, I am going to take you up to the front. You need to be sitting on the front pew." I spoke to the grandmother and met several other family members. The boys went to view the body. The middle boy could not leave the casket. I saw him leaning over into the casket crying uncontrollably. Service started and the Praise Team sang one song. Meanwhile, I was watching, *why are they allowing this child to still lean into the casket?* The minister got up, gave the scripture and prayer, this child was still leaning into the casket! Finally, I had enough! I walked up to the casket removed the child, then sat him down next to his brothers. I knew this was going to be a hard fight.

The Youngest Son

Again, I was mostly concerned about Samuel; school had started and I made sure he was there. His pain could be felt. Already, other students teased him chanting, "What is this mama's boy going to do?" As cruel as the statement was I compassionately wondered the same thing. I followed Samuel closely for the next few months. Then, he stopped attending school. Shortly thereafter, I received some shocking news— Samuel had been arrested. But, he did not commit the crime, his cousin did and left him to take the wrap. The police came to the Samuel's house and he did not run, there was no reason to. The police questioned, booked and later released him with a court date. I thought everything was alright especially when he kept saying, "I'll tell them the truth, I didn't do it!" The only problem was he would not say who did the crime. He thought if the law knew he was innocent, everything would be alright! Samuel refused to tell who was responsible following the streets, *no stitch rule.*

I appeared in court to testify on Samuel's behalf. The judge on the case was emphatic about someone paying for this crime! Through his plea of innocence, the judge sentenced him to five years in prison. Whoa, my heart was aching! Tragically, the youngest son was off to prison. Samuel stayed in touched. We sent his school work and within two years— he graduated. The correctional institution gave me permission to present Samuel with his Travis Academy diploma. The correctional officers were very nice, they allowed us to take pictures. It was a great day of celebration for 50 young men who received their diploma or trade certificate. For Samuel it was a happy moment in June of 2006 because high school was completed!

Over the next three years, we communicated with Samuel encouraging him to get involved in positive activities and stay close to the Lord. Remarkably, he became choir leader and chaplain assistant, God showed him favor. It was nothing to receive a phone call from him in prison. Once I got on the phone, one of the correctional officers would say, "I got Samuel here and he wants to talk to you."

The Protective Hand of God

When Samuel was released, he headed straight to Travis Academy. It was both happy and sad time. Happy for his freedom, but sad this young man spent five years imprisoned for a crime someone else committed. Samuel began to tell me about his activities and various roles over that time. He was healthy, his skin was looking good and gained some weight. He studied the bible like [never] before; his use of scriptures was indicative of numerous hours spent in God's word. It was refreshing to hear him talk about various people, who God strategically placed in his life. He had taken up a trade earning his certificates in horticulture and landscaping. Each Sunday he participated in the worship service and given special privileges, such as leading bible study with the other men. The more he talked, the more I thought about the blessings that occurred from incarceration.

My mind took flight about the awesome God we served. Samuel had no support, no place to live, no money and no job before he went to prison. I was upset at first, once I put everything in perspective I realized God took him from central city Milwaukee, where he was homeless, lived in the middle of a drug infested neighborhood and placed him in an institution where he learned Christ personally.

Upon his release, there was a strong foundation in Christ. He could have been abused, misused and strung out on drugs in the neighborhood where he lived. But God removed him and made a safe haven inside the walls of a prison. Who would have thought God would operate like that? His protective hands worked for Samuel because he was unjustly removed from the community. Like Joseph in Genesis 50:20, *But as for you* [you in this case meaning society], *ye thought evil against me; but God meant it unto good.* Supporting families in crisis was what we had to do. I called it 360 degrees of service. Some people have said, "Dorothy you give too much," but I would say, "Who can out give God?" He has done so much for me and when the Spirit instructs me, it is the least I can do.

TOMS
(TIPS ON MOVING STUDENTS)

POTENTIAL   PERFORMANCE

- *Don't be shocked by the words of students, allow your words to change the dynamics*
- *Students need support during death and grieving*
- *Communication with agencies can help bridge the gap*

CHAPTER NINETEEN

AN UNFORUNATE TURN

Life can take a turn for the worse in a matter of minutes. The Department of Public Instruction (DPI) sent a letter in October of 2014 informing us that the school's auditor turned in our documentation late and DPI was removing our schools from the Milwaukee Parental Choice Program (MPCP). Astonished, as I read the letter, it stated we could appeal. We tried reaching out to them— the only response we received was seek legal counsel. Not one single communication between our school and DPI was helpful. When citizens are late with their federal taxes, they receive a fine, they do not get kicked out of the country. What harsh treatment I thought, but this is still America. No one knew what to do, this had never happened before. The information was shared with our board and other individuals; we needed recommendations for lawyers—I knew this would be a fight. Instantly, my mind reflected on one dynamic administrator in the program Tracy Laster. She worked hard to meet the demands of DPI, sadly her physical health failed. The stress was too much, and this brilliant leader had a stroke and her school closed.

A law firm was recommended, and we made contact to set up a meeting. This lawyer was livid about the evil actions of MPCP and DPI. After some negotiations, they issued some unreasonable ultimatums. One, we would never be late, again. Consequently, the next two requests were more devastating. DPI stated we must give up our right to appeal and secure a surety bond. I had never heard of this when you were considered financially solvent. Curious, I said to DPI, "I thought a surety bond was for people having financial difficulty and why do we have to get one?" Their response was that I was correct, but because we were late, they get to set the punishment. And then I was told our bond had to be a quarter of one year's revenue.

Clearly, the DPI had no sympathy for the children, staff or vendors caught in the crossfire or concern about their welfare. Both Travis Academy and Travis Technology High Schools were in the program, that meant two sureties bonds for a combined total of $1.1 million dollars. Our attorney told us maybe we could get November's payment and if we could not, I should close the schools. "God will not allow Travis Academy to close, not now," I told her while I sat in her office. "For nearly 18 years we have been servicing children from grades K4-12 and we will continue." The agreement was sent and reluctantly we signed it. We really had no choice, or they would put us out of the MPCP. We had a difficult time raising the bond money. While this occurred, supposedly DPI leaked to the news— we may close. The newspaper jumped on the story *like white on rice* digging up every negative story it could. God blessed our schools and I knew that He was with us, but we were attacked from every hand. One article written by a journalist who failed to understand— improperly reported my salary breakdown hinting a higher than normal salary. In the interview, I was transparent and told the journalist that the school owed me back money from when my 401K and mutual funds were cashed to save the school from financial setbacks. Non- profits are public records and I shared the information with the reporter. The journalist disclosed this in small print knowing people would never focus on the pay back, but the total amount.

I felt like Job in the bible who was under attack by the enemy. Job was an upright man and trusted servant of the Lord. Job lost everything and that was exactly how I felt.

My church prayed fervently for me—friends and relatives were praying, also. My Aunt Pearl prayed with me, we have a very close relationship. Aunt Pearl believed in her special connection to heaven. She would say, "I'm not bragging but it's going to be okay because I know I can get a prayer through!" Sometimes, things happen in life, not just for me but for someone else. Other schools needed to know you must be willing to fight for what is right. The state's mind was already made up on which low performing schools they wanted to close. What do I mean? They wanted students to be proficient, but it was problematic just to get at- risk students to school. The undertaking was totally different. There was no strong family structure, financial resources and numerous other issues as well. Moreover, we had ninth graders reading at fourth grade level. Children were born into circumstances that no one in the DPI had been exposed to. They were supposed to be educated and compassionate people. It was a success to us when students improved from fourth to fifth grade level. But the department wants them to improve instantly. Yet, our children faced abuse, hunger, violence, homelessness, abandonment issues, other emotional and behavioral problems. The kind of things that I dedicated my life to serving the underprivileged, neglected and ignored. I emptied my savings and investments to start the school and now emptying it again to keep the school open. Like Job my philosophy was …the *Lord gave and the Lord has taken away, blessed be the name of the Lord!* (Job 1:21) It was disgraceful that the newspaper refused to look for good in our community. We pulled children from the back rooms of houses, homeless situations and brought them into a caring environment they would not have otherwise known. The newspaper seemed not to care that we had students on probation or parole being educated in our schools. They did not care that our mission was 360 degrees of service and we abided by that. I cannot count the number of times we [collectively] helped parents beyond educational needs such as rent, groceries or going to court with families to support them. DPI was determined to close us, but what we represented and poured into this community could never be closed.

By December's deadline, the bond amount for the schools was met with $789,000 what an amazing God we serve! The bank loaned us $700,000 and I gave the bank $100,000 of personal money from my 401K to continue serving the community. We closed Travis Tech High because we could not raise the bond. We asked DPI for additional time, but unfortunately it was denied. A letter arrived from DPI stating our extension was denied and they were closing the school, everyone was on Christmas break. Almost immediately, DPI sent letters to parents of tech high students concerning this action. The staff quickly worked with parents to complete applications for the Academy because this campus was K4-12 grades. Thankfully, most of our students joined us at the Academy and we hired many of the teachers from tech high.

In Mark 11:24 [paraphrased] it says that whatsoever you ask, when you pray, believe that you receive them, and you will have them. I was believing God to help us through these struggling times. In my heart, this thought arose, *What should we do next?*

The Battle Goes On

The battle was not over; we needed a new attorney. Our accountant recommended a law firm that could possibly help. At the law office, I met with Attorney Jennifer Walther to discuss an action plan to correct the injustices against our school. The staff and parents rallied together to make our school days successful. Honestly, I was blessed by our parents who came out to lend their support. We called several PTO meetings where I attempted to explain new developments. My integrity was put on the line and I did not want parents confused about what the newspaper misrepresented. I wanted to explain in person, face to face and heart to heart. Each time I tried a to give an account, parents would comment, "Dr. Travis you don't have to explain to us. We have been with you long enough to know that you would not do anything to hurt the students or the school." Another parent said, "Your track record is known, and they don't know you will take your money and give it to all of us." The PTO's vice president spoke up and told the group. "I have been evicted and Dr. Travis has helped my family. She went to court with me and my child and I know she went to court with others." Humbly speaking, I was appreciative of the comments, but I still wanted to explain to parents my side. One told me, "We love you, and believe in you." They all agreed. We carried on with the evening's agenda. Many of them struggled— and still wanted to send caring messages to the community about the school's great work serving at risk children and how we made a difference. We took this opportunity to ban together, become stronger and prepare to fight the enemy.

Trust the Lord

We should really trust God— practice stepping out on faith and be patience for His will. I cannot begin to tell you how rough it was after the DPI's unjust decision and try to make one payment to the next. I had to remind myself of biblical times when the Israelites traveled to the promise land, God fed them daily and He would do the same for us.

We struggled the reminder of the year and the Lord kept us. The word says that if we delight ourselves in the Lord, He gives us the desires of our hearts (Psalm 34). Our attorney filed the appeal while we continued to operate until another curve ball was thrown from DPI. We were saving money to adopt some new reading materials and restructure the middle school program. Another report arrived from DPI citing we owed $165, 000 from the audit. The letter came weeks before the required state payment and DPI demanded payment before we received any funds. Now what? There were no more resources. I simply said, "God it is in Your hands."

An Unexpected Blessing

A few days later, I was in my office and my assistant, Ms. Manisha Gaston brought me some materials to review. Out of nowhere, she politely said, "Dr. Travis if you can't find anyone to borrow the money from, I know someone who will let you have it." That shocked me, "You do?" I told her I would give my answer later. We continued to put out fillers in the community for financial assistance. Our financial packaged was ready for anyone willing to do business with us, but to no avail. The next morning after my eyes opened, I conversed with the Lord about hitting a brick wall with no place to go; no one to help. The Holy Spirit reminded me of what Ms. Gaston said the week before. Negative thoughts tried to enter my mind, but I contacted her anyway.

I made it to work and spoke to Ms. Gaston concerning the person who could possibly help the school. She said, "I will contact him." This person agreed. She set up a meeting at 10:00 AM the following day, which left me on pins and needles the night before. The next morning, I informed my staff that I was expecting a gentleman and please do not have him wait, bring him directly to my office. God was sending us my angel. At precisely 10: 00 AM, this amazing man walked through the door with an incredible smile. As he sat down he said, "Manisha Gaston, your assistant said to be sure to wear a suit, but I only own two suits. One suit for funerals and the other one for weddings." My focus was not on his clothes. The more he talked, the more I knew this was the hand of God. He shared that he saved some money for a dedicated project that never materialized and had some available cash in the bank. After hearing about our dilemma, this gentleman told me that he needed to help and revealed his mother did not know about the generous loan. Finally, he introduced himself, "I'm Eugene Bonner." Soon it dawned on me, he was the same person who provided the repast for one of our student who tragically died in a car crash. The parents were financially unable to supply food and Mr. Bonner catered the whole thing- free of charge. He operated a food service company along with several other business ventures. The meeting concluded and Mr. Bonner said that my assistant could work with him once the loan paperwork was drawn up. Now we were in position to pay the Department of Public Instruction (DPI). In Psalms 23:5, it says in part, *You prepare a table before me in the presence of my enemies.* God truly delivered.

Our school semester was finally over. Eighteen years of service and we spent the summer with attorneys to hopefully try to reverse the DPI's decision. The courts were slow moving. We waited for its decision and our attorney kept us informed. In September another school year started with our audit filed on time. Good news came our way, the court decided DPI's treatment was unfair and we won our case! In other words, we could reopen Travis Tech High and the surety bond was cancelled. Unfortunately, the victory was short lived, the DPI appealed the decision and we found ourselves in court again. Meanwhile our auditor had a negative experience going back and forth with DPI because they were not satisfied with the audit. DPI insisted we get another firm and start from scratch. This extreme tactic forced us to hire another company, which was very expensive— DPI left us no choice. We had until the first day of March with only a small window of time to produce a satisfactory audit. By the end of February, we had the firm, all the documents needed and our audit submitted by the deadline. We believed that everything was fine. However, without our knowledge, the auditor notified DPI and told someone the audit would arrive one day late. Apparently, the auditor believed his conversation with DPI was sufficient. They never approved the auditor's request to file to the report one day after. It was not long before we received a letter saying they were rejecting the late audit. This meant no funding for us, they would not so much as look at any of our expenditures for the year. They wanted the entire 1.7 million dollars issued returned and refused to disperse May's payment of $617,000.

Distraught by these events, that night I asked God, "What kind of mean spirited people work in the MPCP office?" If the auditor called and requested a one -day extension, what kind of human being would neglect to inform him of procedures or offer helpful information. We talked to a supervisor from the accounting firm. The auditor was shocked that DPI rejected the audit. We got caught in the middle. Financially, we had to figure out how to make it through the end of the year. I secured some loans from some individuals in the community to meet April's expenses. Although I had many promises for the month of May, I was unsuccessful securing money for May's payroll. Our attorney was busy working on a special injunction that would require them to pay for May. The attorney's efforts proved to be futile. Payroll was ready to be submitted, but there was no funding. We were at the end of 19 years and things were not looking good. We had to lay everybody off. Most of the staff were laid off in May, then rest of them in June. The only thing left functioning was our volunteer office staff. I said, "Wow Lord, what a year!" A group of ten staff members decided to sue the school and my name was included in the lawsuit for their last paycheck— this put me in a dark place. I went to God with this supplication:

Dear Lord, I thought the staff understood that DPI did not pay us our May payment. There is no way we could pay them until we got some money. I am really confused; do they think I was not going to pay them? The problem is we have no money. The lawsuit infers that I have no intentions on paying them. Lord, I thought my staff understood me because if I had any money, they would get it first. I cried out to God for mercy.

The Finale

Over the summer the Board of Directors met, and we grappled between continuing the choice program, becoming independent or closing our doors. When September of 2016 rolled around, it marked 20 years of serving the community. We decided to refer parents to another school. We worked with seniors to complete their graduating year. We ultimately decided to be a private school for a short time. The DPI sent a letter telling us that we were officially banned from the program. I would like to think since we started Ceria M. Travis on December 2, 1996, that I would use December 2, 2016 as the official closing date. The only thing was our students did not want to graduate that early. After the holiday season, we held the graduation ceremony on January 26, 2017. It was a very special moment as the last 11 students received their high school diplomas. In the words of one graduate who said, "I thank Travis Academy, for without it who knows where I would be." A bittersweet moment ended a long era of educational service.

TOMS
(TIPS ON MOVING STUDENTS)

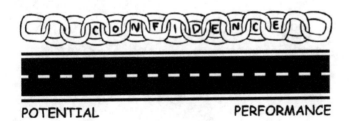

POTENTIAL   PERFORMANCE

- *Learn to be thankful for doors closed, but avoid an angry heart*
- *The generosity of angels can calm a storm and allow progress to continue*
- *Knowing the political climates can be useful*

CHAPTER TWENTY

The LORD IS MY SHEPHERD

I have shared numerous stories about my students, to bring faces to children and emotion to the heart, however I want every reader to grasp what is currently happening in this country relating to at risk children. Last year, according to Build On.org, a program for at-risk students the study concludes there are 1.2 million students who dropped out of high school every year, which is an outrage! One is too many and one million is a national crisis. The National Report Card for students, states boys drop out of school faster than girls and African American boys drop out at a higher rate than other ethnic groups.

National Center for Children in Poverty (NCCP) reported that about 15 million children under 18 live in poverty today. Study after study correlates poor education with race and poverty—frankly without change, the system will continue to fail. The paradigm is not a one size fits all, the approach must be strategic and intentional to meet the needs of every child. Certain factors affect the education of children. After many years in education I have witnessed that every aspect of the student's life is affected by their environment and poverty creates one of the biggest obstacles to learning. Poverty or not, several factors exist that I believe are cautionary indications that students will not be successful in school.

To shift students from potential to performance level; the at -risk child must recognize that we as educators, parents and the community believe in them and we must find better ways to support and improve education in America.

Listed below are social and emotional dynamics that can affect a child's ability to learn, I will refer to them as *The Dangerous Dozen:*

- Low Self –Esteem
- Inability to Resolve Conflict
- Hostile School Climate
- High Suspension Rate
- Outdated Curriculum
- Ineffective Parenting
- Poor Home and School Attitude
- Peer Pressure
- Criminal Behavior
- Lack of Community Support
- Failure to Dream
- Feeling Emotionally Invisible and Isolated

The role we play as educators in the lives of children is an [all] important one. We must keep our children engaged, encouraged and loved. We can never give up on them. If we do, the tone is set for future generations that would be too costly for society to bear. It is imperative that we understand their weaknesses and turn those weaknesses into strengths. In my early days, I became a door knocker, in my case it was literal, but I am speaking figuratively here. What does this mean? I mean knock on doors for better education, create improvements and walk students into fulfillment of hopes and dreams. You might not arrive early like some educators the moment the engineer unlocks the building or you might not visit homes like I did, but there must be a fighting spirit inside of you that will rise up with righteous indignation when government sacrifices education for prisons and wars, when money is not equally dispersed to children born in poverty, when parents beat children down because they themselves were beat down or when you see untapped potential buried because every child learns differently. We educators are on the front lines and we must step in to fight for innocent children who cannot speak or protect themselves and create a refuge for them, even if it is only a few hours each day.

One of the first scriptures I learned was Psalms 23:1, *The Lord is my shepherd, I shall not want.* As an educator, it reminds me how God protects me, leads me, He restores me, while going through the deepest valley. In the field of education there will always be successes and failures. And I think no one wants to feel they have let children down, but sometimes its society's evils that swallows them whole.

My reflections come from love, love for educating children. I was sitting still—silent, and my mind reflected over the years. I thought about the grandmother who insisted that I accept her grandson into my new school. I thought about the students who are still in business. I thought about students who I know that still work in corporations making six figure salaries and yes, I thought about the ones who went to prison. I thought about the ones who died young. I thought about, did we answer the Lord's call? I thought about the person who would always say to me, "I pray for you Dr. Travis daily because you are such an encouragement to us but who encourages you?" I thought about the parent who handed me with a box of handmade soaps with a note attached that said:

Dr. Travis, thank you for always believing in me and for the unconditional love and support you have always given to my family. I pray God continue to bless you. You have been a blessing to me since the first day I met you. I will forever be grateful for God placing you in me and my kids' lives. These words really touched and encouraged my heart, it is with great humility I receive these words as evidence of God's grace.

When the Lord is your shepherd, you worry less about life challenges because they come without permission or invitation, they come unexpectedly and most times they are unwanted. Challenges will do one of two things, either they will strengthen your faith in God or weaken you to the world. I found myself standing at crossroads of my faith, a faith in God that was built from many years of believing in His word. Yet, my own faith being tested like never before. Its very foundation shaken like a mild earthquake that caused minimal damage, but damage nonetheless. The aftermath left me with a few questions for God; I surely could not answer. How could this be? What am I going to do? But the real question was, "What are you going to do God?" I knew what I had to do, I had to pray more, believe more and be still to really know He is God. Then, listen enough to hear God's gentle voice and receive divine guidance. Travis Academy's fate was at stake. The future of at risk students, the faculty, and administrators were in jeopardy. Hoping for the best, while preparing for the worst changed my perspective. Facing this Goliath made me realize there are no perfect schools, but there is a perfect God. God halted my tracks and caused me to re-examine everything. His promises of grace, mercy, humility and love was placed under the microscope of my heart for safe-keeping and reassurance, so during these tough times I would be able to function. God had NOT forsaken me!

What God called me to do for children comes from a place of passion and love. A passion released early in my life when I was not looking— and from love God had already placed in my heart. Everything built, and everything labored for the Lord had started to crumble right in front of me. He allowed this to happen. Why? This question along with many others began to occupy my thoughts daily. However, the focus had to be turned away from what man could not do—to what God could. Even with a slight decline in faith—my expectations did not completely suffer because I knew enough about God's word to stand on it, no matter how the situation appeared. The Lord took me through this process for a reason. As an educator, you should be objective, receptive and caring. However, as a child of the King you should be obedient, humble and faithful; these are the attributes that moves God's heart. This ordeal taught me waiting for God was and still is an intricate part of His plan to bring me out from beneath the ashes. Patience really is a virtue and we must let it have its perfect work.

Fulfilling purpose does not exempt anyone from trouble, it does not mean for you to try to figure out the solution and get ahead of God. It means for you to trust Him completely. Oftentimes, we want to take matters in our own hands only to the detriment of ourselves and sometimes others. God thoughts are not our thoughts, nor His ways our ways. Gaining wisdom through trials will take you further— experience may not always be the best teacher—for some learning can come simply by hearing the testimony of someone else. I hope my testimony or experiences will cause you to grow! The physical doors of Ceria M Travis Academy are now closed, but my voice is not and the door to the hearts of many remain open along with my love for a population of students the world wants to throw away will continue throughout eternity.

TOMS
(TIPS ON MOVING STUDENTS)

POTENTIAL   PERFORMANCE

- *The only evidences we have of life is growth*
- *Help students grow*
- *It is not over until the students WIN*

PART THREE

CHAPTER TWENTY-ONE

Finished But Not Finished

When I concluded chapter twenty just a few short years ago, I had no idea that a pandemic would hit and turn our world upside down. Talking about flipping the script, that's an understatement when it comes to education and the classroom. It seems like we have been in a whirlwind of communication and action that still is mind boggling. The question is what are we going to do? I have had the opportunity to work in a variety of school buildings since that time: facilitating team meetings, consulting with administrators, substituting for teachers and instructing middle school students. The conversation between virtual learning and traditional classroom setting continued to be a discussion at both the local and national level. My hope is that we do not lose many students in the process of dealing with COVID-19 and the variation of its strands as well as other viruses.

As we faced this pandemic, we understood that it was vibrantly alive in the thousands of communities, not only in America but other communities around our world. Each news announcement reminded us that this was not a momentary problem but one that required us to stay on lockdown for over a year. The wearing of mask was a national mandate and I watched as children placed them over their months and noses wondering what is this strange disease we need protection from. None of us knew, we lived in constant fear waiting for answers. A middle school boy walked in a classroom and said that his mother was in the hospital as well as his grandfather. He stated that both were on ventilators and facing deaths from COVID-19. With tears in his eyes, he asked 'when will it all end?" I observed a nurse informing a teacher that 6 students in her class would be out because of Covid-19 and there were seven other who were quarantined. "We don't want to get it" was the cry of several other in that class as the nurse exited. The nurse shouted, "I hope not". Since the opportunity presented itself, the teacher and I shared hope with the students. I feel it's our duties to encourage and be a support system for our children during these critical times. When I think of the losses this virus has created, it is not just related to learning, but it is related to death, loss of jobs, housing, finances, and emotional stability. I am encouraging each of us to take the time to walk through some of the pain our students are facing doing this difficult time.

The Coronavirus has changed our lives forever and educators continue to make adjusts in ways that maximize learning. Our children have faced new and uncertain territories, but with guidance and tenacity they will survive. As the years progress. I believe children all over our nation will tell their stories. For the first time, many students faced virtual learning and they struggled with organizing eight hours of daily study while mom and dad went to work. Let's not forget the students with little or no internet connection and they fail to complete assignments; worrying that they may not pass to the next grade. They missed their friends, teachers and their learning environment as they had known it. These will be stories of fear, isolation, confusion, displacement, and God knows what else. It will be many years before we completely measure the effects of this virus on our children. My message to you remains the same. Don't give up! Adapt, Adjust, and Affirm their value as a learner in your classroom. You are a big part of their success.

I know this pandemic will come to an end and we will have forever a "new normal". Life will not be the same, but I challenge you to continue giving the children your absolute BEST. Affirming who they are was demonstrated as one school in the mid-south created energy for daily learning by reciting this simple poem: I AM ME.

I am Me,

I am One,

I can't do everything,

But I can do some things,

And what I can Do,

I MUST do,

And with GOD's Help,

I Will Do!

You may use this Affirmation poem at any time. Or select others!

As we move forward in this 21st century of learning, I have additional food for thought that you became familiar with in the other chapters. Here are your tips on moving students from potential to performance. Here are your TOMS.

TOMS
(TIPS ON MOVING STUDENTS)

POTENTIAL   PERFORMANCE

- *Pay close attention to the mental health of our children*
- *Plan activities that focus on the mind*
- *Practice careful listening skills, COVID-19 demands a listening alert*
- *Promote relaxation- teach children to just breathe.*
- *Probe deeper if you think a healthcare professional is needed.*
- *Prepare lessons that not only raise test scores but raise consciousness of students*
- *Promise to be there for them and keep your promise.*
- *Pray for our children*

GUIDE QUESTIONS

"Think It Through"

I have developed 21 situational questions that cover problems teachers may experience. Being aware of problems that one school is experiencing may possibly help another school to prevent a similar situation. Also, it may help you as an individual instructor to see the variety of behaviors that people exhibit. This can teach and reinforce thinking and understanding that solutions to problems may differ. As an educator you want to always come up with the best solution possible for your school.

You may write your comments on the space provided or have a verbal conversation with a friend/group or simply think about it in a way that will encourage you to better serve your students.

QUESTION #1

Most of your students failed the last two geography tests. You are unhappy with their results. Upon investigating, you discover that vocabulary is a problem. Students confessed that they marked any answers because they didn't understand the meaning of many words. Students ask you" what does confide mean and what does illustrate mean? The list goes on and on. The department chair tells you the schedule does not allow time for vocabulary teaching. Your students cannot fail another test.

Think it through

_____

_____

_____

_____

_____

QUESTION #2

You have a conversation with another teacher about one of her students not making progress. The student hears your conversation and reports to parents that you are making negative suggestions to his teacher. Parents become angry and demand a meeting with the administrator. Administrator holds a conference without your presence. Later, you receive a letter of reprimand but tell you not to worry. However, you still want to tell your side.

Think it through

_____

_____

_____

_____

_____

QUESTION #3

Your 8th grade student has improved in reading this year, by one grade level. You are grateful for the relationship you are building with him. He has the first meeting with his high school counselor today. Problem is he does not have transportation. You are driving to the high school at that time. School policy is "don't ride students in your car". Can you help?

Think it through

_____

_____

_____

_____

_____

QUESTION #4

You have a student competing in the citywide Dr. Martin Luther King Jr. Speech Contest. On Monday morning of the competition, the student shows up wearing the same clothes that he wore on Friday. He stated that his mother got drunk and had a fight with him, and he slept in the park all weekend. Your mind is racing. He cannot go to the competition looking like that!

Think it through

_____

_____

_____

_____

_____

QUESTION #5

You would like to make a presentation to the school for Black History Month. You ask your principal for permission, he states he will get back to you. Two weeks have passed and you still have not heard from him. You sent a note asking permission again. He responds, "I didn't forget I'll get back with you". There is only one week left in the month.

Think it through

_____

_____

_____

_____

_____

QUESTION #6

This student has not been to school for ten days and the phone is disconnected. You want to reach out to the parent, but this student lives on a rough side of town. Yet you cannot shake her from your memory and you would like to check on her.

Think it through

_____

_____

_____

_____

_____

QUESTION #7

Every sport in the school is recognized via the PA system, except yours. You work with the girls' teams. You hear them announce the results of the boys' football, basketball and soccer games. Nothing is ever announced about the girls and their basketball team having a winning season. This upsets you!

Think it through

_____

_____

_____

_____

_____

QUESTION #8

Last three weeks you have been called during your prep time to substitute for another teacher. You are angry about it, however you smile and go on. Next week you think certainly it's going to be somebody else's turn because several other teachers have prep time the same as yours! Again, the office assigns you to substitute doing your prep time. You greatly dislike their decision.

Think it through

_____

_____

_____

_____

_____

QUESTION #9

You are a first-year teacher assigned to teach English Language Art. You have prepared all summer. You attended new teachers in-service and everything went well. The entire staff returns for in-service training and another teacher has an assignment to teach Math this year and rumor is she's not happy. The next day you get a notice that you are no longer teaching English, you are teaching Math. Your heart sinks but you're not sure what to do.

Think it through

_____

_____

_____

_____

_____

QUESTION #10

A fight breaks out with one of the special education students, he is out of control. The police are called and the administrator is present. You are the special education teacher who wants to intervene and de-escalate the situation because you know the student. But the administrator says you are not needed and do not interfere. You are crushed because your specialized training is for cases like this.

Think it through

_____

_____

_____

_____

_____

QUESTION #11

A teacher has been successful in developing a curriculum for students for 12 years. Her test scores go high. She has now moved to a new school, but it's the same grade level and the same subject. She wants to use her curriculum. But the school is telling her she must use their district-wide curriculum. She is not happy with that decision.

Think it through

QUESTION #12

It is time to decorate for the holidays. The theme is given to you by the administration. Everyone in your section would like to do something different. You asked permission to select your own theme! Your request is denied and everyone received an email stating in harsh terms either you comply or forfeit the opportunity. Everyone feels belittled and upset.

Think it through

QUESTION #13

Your school district has issued a timeline for the completion of a science project. Due to the time restriction, it is unlikely that your students will do a good job. Other staff members tell you not to be concerned with unfinished projects. The concern is about quality work. Requesting an extension of two weeks would allow your students to be more successful. Your colleagues are unsupportive of this measure.

Think it through

_____

_____

_____

_____

_____

QUESTION #14

Your past working relationship with one of the teachers has been difficult. It is obvious that she dislikes you. She is the chair of the Honor Roll Committee. Your students' names were omitted from the first marking period honors list. She claimed it was an accident. For the second honors list the names of your students were misspelled. She apologized for the error. This time she pushed you too far. You have lost your patience with this teacher.

Think it through

_____

_____

_____

_____

QUESTION #15

A special education student asked his teacher for paper to draw on. She agreed to his request but informed him that he has to complete his classwork first. He gets angry with the teacher and stomps on her foot. The student is suspended. An IEP meeting will be scheduled to consider if placement is correct. The teacher is second-guessing her decision. She wonders if she did the right thing by telling him to wait until he completed his assignment instead of giving him paper to draw and keep him quiet. This teacher has mixed feelings. Did she do the right thing?

Think it through

_____

_____

_____

_____

_____

QUESTION #16

A teacher comes to school upset from an argument with her abusive husband. She starts teaching class and students are not focused on the lesson. She told one student three times to sit down and the student refused. The teacher reacted in anger, throwing a water bottle at the student. The administrator wants to fire for unprofessional behavior, and her potential danger to students. Remorsefully, she explained her situation to the administrator, and he is thinking about her situation as well. Help them out.

Think it through

_____

_____

_____

_____

QUESTION #17

A teacher wants to provide help to students suffering from emotional instability after the pandemic. He starts a new group called the Be Encouraged Group (BEG) using the Bible as the book for instructions. The school tells him that he cannot use the Bible. He is unhappy with the decision.

Think it through

_____

_____

_____

_____

_____

QUESTION #18

Think about the child that is doing well in school. You have their daily routine. Are there any additional ways you can encourage the students?

Think it through

_____

_____

_____

_____

_____

QUESTION #19

Think about the student who exhausts you to the point that if they did not show up for school it would not really matter to you. Write down the name of that student. How can you be an encouragement?

Think it through

_____

_____

_____

_____

_____

QUESTION #20

One of your students lost his 14-year-old brother to gun violence. Your student comes to school depressed. The family is struggling to pay for their child's funeral expenses. The student is weighing heavily on your mind. Perhaps you could do something for him and his family.

Think it through

_____

_____

_____

_____

_____

QUESTION #21

You want to build a better relationship with your students. You reflect on several missed opportunities to serve them. You want next year to be better.

Think it through

_____

_____

_____

_____

_____

I Woke Up This Morning

I woke up this morning with love in my heart. A day of safety is what I want for my students.

I woke up this morning with inspiration on my mind. Some child will need to be encouraged today.

I woke up this morning with a desire to overcome fear today. Some child had a bad experience last night. Perhaps it was an unhealthy parent interaction or abuse or violence or depression. When they look in my eyes they must see hope.

I woke up this morning and said, this is the day that GOD has made. I will teach so my students will learn.

I woke up this morning recognizing that a peaceful day is my goal. It's what I want for all the students to achieve.

I woke up this morning knowing there may be some problems, but striving for solutions is a MUST.

I woke up determined to give my best, for when I give my best, my students will know and be glad, I will know and be grateful. **GOD** will know, and **BE GLORIFIED**.

—_Dorothy Travis Moore_

Other Written Works by
Dorothy Travis Moore

Where is a Caring God When I Need Him?
Copyright 2005

I Have Prayer for You Come Holy Spirit
Copyright 2004

Come Holy Spirit
Copyright 2004

Wisdom from Above
Copyright 2003

The Light Book of Soul Script
Copyright 1976

ABOUT THE AUTHOR

DOROTHY TRAVIS MOORE has brought a unique richness to her educational journey for over 35 years. She founded Travis Academy in December 1996 and served as its President and CEO with 20 years of devoted service to this organization helping at risk students find their potential and place in society.

Her educational background has produced many different titles and roles as Principal, Administrator, Special Education Teacher, Therapist, Businesswoman, and Minister gaining the attention and respect from leaders, peers, students and the community. Dorothy also served as a National Educational Consultant with the prestigious National School Safety Center working as their advocate to promote a secure, safe, peaceful and nurturing environment for children.

Dorothy uses another platform as motivational speaker to bring awareness to her field of expertise in handling at risk students and has shared her message to national and international audiences. Her belief is everyone has a purpose in life, and we must work hard to fulfill the purpose set before us, especially if it includes working with the at-risk or challenged students.

Some of the awards she has received are Top Principal of Leadership, Who's Who Among Executives and Professionals in the United States, University of Wisconsin Distinguished Alumni Award and the Alpha Kappa Alpha Central Regional Director's Outstanding Educator Award to name a few. These many honors chronicle a lifetime spent addressing the needs of children and families who live with financial and emotional instability.

This pioneer woman has enjoyed her passion to educate students over the years, but states that her greatest accomplishment comes from helping children and families! One hundred years from now nobody will care about the type of house you lived in, or the kind of car you drove. What will matter is, *"Did you make a difference in the lives of children?"*

For more information about workshops, lectures and other speaking engagements, contact her in one of the following ways:

Email: *dtravismoore@yahoo.com*
Website: *https://dorothytravismoore.com/*

CPSIA information can be obtained
at www.ICGtesting.com
Printed in the USA
BVHW032324051022
648676BV00005B/12